MOVING ICEBERGS

Leading people to lasting change

Steve Patty, Ph.D.

DIALOGUES IN ACTION, LLC
WWW.DIALOGUESINACTION.COM

To my friend, Janet.

Dialogues In Action, LLC
408 NW 12th Avenue, Suite 506
Portland, OR 97209

© 2012 by Steve Patty, Ph.D
All Rights Reserved.
ISBN 978-0-9852971-0-7

TABLE OF CONTENTS

INTRODUCTION

I t sounds like the prologue to an old lounge joke: A priest, two ministers, and a rabbi walk into a room and sit down around a table. But this real-life meeting one day in 1887 launched an enterprise of social action that has spanned more than 120 years and touched practically every major community across North America. These four men came together initially to address Denver's social problems and ended up founding what is today one of the world's most recognized charities, the United Way.

Over the years the United Way has marshaled an immense trove of resources toward community development. It stewards $4 billion annually in an effort to catalyze social improvement in families, neighborhoods, and cities across North America. The scale of its investment, however, is more than matched by the scope of its work. To "mobilize the caring power of communities" is an enormous task, especially when the work extends across a continent. Can you imagine?

How do you intervene at points of inscrutable social vulnerability and intractable social ill which, in some cases, have been embedded in communities for generations? How do you target areas of local, regional, and national influence to make a true and lasting difference in people? How do you mobilize whole communities to shoulder the responsibility of truly caring for the welfare of their neighbors, regardless of gender, ethnicity, generation, religion, or orientation?

These challenges occupy the mind of United Way's CEO, Brian Gallagher. He has been at the helm since 2001, navigating the tumult of charitable venture and vicissitude. In a moment of revealing self-awareness during a 2008 interview with the *Washington Post*, Gallagher surprised the nonprofit community by admitting, "Despite spending millions to support scores of local programs, the 121-year-old United Way has not made measureable progress on these core problems. The country's social safety net is broken and the United Way must redirect its money toward the root causes and hold itself accountable."

Causing change in human systems is formidable work. Gallagher and his colleagues at the United Way are not alone in finding it so. At times, difference-making eludes even the best efforts of the most gifted leaders and the most storied social enterprises. At some point, it will confound each one of us interested in touching the lives of others. Securing true and lasting human change is neither simple nor easy. As Gallagher observes, people are filled with tough and seemingly endless *core problems* and *root causes*. Progress requires that we change more than the circumstances and situations *surrounding* people. If there are core problems and root causes, then the core and root parts embedded *within* people need to be changed— things like beliefs, values, positions, leanings, hopes, premises, fears, and commitments. Those *within* parts are much trickier to access and usually much more difficult to renovate than any situation or circumstance surrounding a person.

If the essential power for true and durable human impact is found in core and root elements, then we have no choice other than to engage those deeper features. Simply improving the situations encasing people will not be enough. Even if we should succeed in renovating, upgrading, or even revolutionizing the structure of a human system, people can still be driven and animated by old core and former root parts. The face of any situation can be changed with no change in the substance of those inhabiting it. We witness, then, the appearance of transformation but none of its true power—a modification of human veneer but not of deeper human material. Our challenge is to find a way to grapple with and intervene in the inner parts of people. That is our best chance of making true impact.

As we think about how to do this in the following pages, we will be using a common metaphor: an iceberg. We will use it in an uncommon way, however. Usually when we talk about making monumental change, we speak of facing giants or moving mountains or something of the sort. Here, we will think in terms of moving icebergs, of turning them and changing their course. But why would any of us want to move an iceberg? There would be no good reason unless, of course, we found ourselves staring at one from the speeding deck of the *Titanic*.

Many of us feel like we are on a version of *Titanic's* deck. We face colleagues and clients that threaten to tear a hole in us (or them) and pull us all under. We face organizations long imperiled by mediocrity and needing to move forward or even just move enough to survive in the shifting currents of social or economic uncertainty. We face people in whom we see great potential but who seem stuck, unable to get out of their own way. We face institutions with habits, cultures, and ways of work that obstruct the way of progress, and we wonder what opportunities will be missed if those organizational features remain unchanged. Some of us, on our more introspective days, face flaws in our own lives that we suspect might rip bright gashes in our legacies as leaders.

An iceberg, in our discussion, represents a human system. It may be an individual human system—an employee, manager, colleague, or client. It might be a larger, more complex human system of people gathered around a mission—an organization, company, department, team, or institution. It could be a familial human system—a family, clan, or community—or a collection of people sharing a particular characteristic that binds them to a similar experience. An iceberg is a human system that is solid, substantial, and buoyant, or filled with empty cavities, drifting aimlessly, and slowly sinking. An iceberg is a human system that is positioned and progressing well, or stuck and in need of dislodging to make way toward a better trajectory and more abundant future.

The iceberg metaphor illustrates a few key traits to the challenge of developing human systems: An iceberg is bigger than it looks on the surface, just as with most challenges of human change. An iceberg's mass lies mostly hidden out of sight, just as with most features of human habit and motivation. Iceberg tips can be cosmetically rearranged by chipping here or there without causing any substantive change to the position of the whole. So also, many efforts to change people lead to mere adjustments of superficial features without true and genuine transformation.

Our work is not just about fixing whatever is wrong, however. We hold a precious stewardship—the privilege of investing in people, helping people, guiding and leading people, opening the way for people to reach their potential and leave a mark on their worlds. We desire to have bold and brilliant impact in their lives and the organizations and communities where they gather, work, and live. Programs that are going well—we want them to go better. Influence we are having—we want it to go deeper. Differences we are making—we want those differences to be more profound and lasting. We want to leave a legacy and do something of significance. We want more than just to touch the tip of the iceberg.

Fundamentally, we believe that people can be moved and that their lives, both individually and collectively, can be turned around. At least on our most hope-filled days, we believe. We also recognize that it will take the right kind of leverage to effect true change. These two attributes are most essential to our iceberg metaphor: (1) the iceberg can be moved no matter how massive and stubborn it appears;

and (2) it will take the right kind of intervention to move it. Herein is both possibility and challenge. The bold attempt to make a difference in a person or community is as daring as trying to move an iceberg.

Before us lies a tremendous task. If we believe people are the most profound expression of our vocations' impact, the most worthy target of our lives' investment, and if we believe people can truly move, turning from where they are now to where they need to be, then how best can it be done? What can we do to help transform human beings and human systems?

Through these pages we will consider a theory of human change. We will walk with individuals and organizations who, like us, desire to do great things in the lives of people. We will think about the fundamental question of how to make a difference in ourselves, in others, and in our human situations—whatever those situations might be.

We will take this challenge in three parts. Part I will introduce a rubric, or model, to orient us and organize our efforts. Part II will take us into the deeper points of leverage and help us know how to develop ourselves and strategically engage others. Part III will unpack some examples of change at work in real-life individuals and organizations. Fundamentally, the intent of this book is to increase our capacity to make a positive impact in the human systems we care about. So, let's dive in.

PART 1

GETTING TO
DEEPER CHANGE

1. CHANGING

Boris Porkovich has his hands full of opportunity. He is the dean of graduate programs in business at the only university in the Principality of Monaco, the famed and beautiful playground for the fabulously wealthy along the Côte d' Azure. The International University of Monaco is a young university—only a few years old in its most recent incarnation—and it's a small university as well. But the faculty and administrators sit poised at an influential nexus of wealth and power along the shimmering edge of the Mediterranean. They aspire to use their unique platform for making a difference in how international business is done. As dean, Porkovich is leading the charge.

He is Australian by nationality, but was recruited from the United States by a visionary French academic, Maxime Crener. He came to academia through an unlikely route of professional rugby, having first competed on the pitch as player and then from the sidelines as coach. In time he left the rough-and-tumble rugby fraternity to join the ranks of higher education administrators. His path wound through administrative stints at universities in Boston and Berkeley and landed him with Crener in the tiny but renowned Principality of Monaco situated at the spectacular intersection of France, Italy, and the Mediterranean Sea.

Porkovich has a knack for propelling people to action. He advances through the corridors of higher education with a potent mix of intellect and charisma. Anyone following him into a lecture hall or through a student cafeteria sees an almost visible pulse of human effect, as if he is still outfitted in rugby uniform and pushing through a scrum. Since he is fluent in four languages, he easily projects his coaching persona to faculty and students who gather from around the world. It's hard to imagine anyone better suited to forging an international graduate school of business into an influential force.

He and his colleagues aim to bring both business acuity and social virtue to the business culture of Monaco and through it to the global marketplace intersecting in the Côte d' Azure. It's a timely task, given the current strains of global economic turmoil. It's also an honorable aim, given the accounts of folly and indiscretion we hear broadcast almost daily about misguided adventurism in the global marketplace. But if it is to be done, it will be accomplished neither through brute, rugby-like force nor the charisma of a coach's persona. If young business leaders are to be developed substantively, then an entire collection of ideas and values will need to be embedded deeply within them. They will have to be inwardly transformed.

For a moment, picture yourself with Porkovich and Crener at the International University of Monaco, designing a strategy to affect business ethos among emerging leaders. Facing an opportunity like this, what would you be thinking about?

How do we create an academic community that will impact the future leaders of international business? How do we help the hearts and minds of young people embrace, embody, and advance the idea of stewardship in business and catalyze similar stewardship in others? How do we form an institution that leverages true and lasting transformation in the business community?

Porkovich and Crener aspire to more than simply building another business school— they figure the world already has plenty. The idea of establishing another iteration of the conventional MBA, even one set on the beautifully riveting Riviera, is insufficient for their dream. Their school needs to take young business professionals who are drawn to the Monegasque Principality and prepare them both to attain the highest levels of profitability and to serve the greater good of humanity. They have to find a way to infuse the two signature staples of business in Monaco—luxury and finance—with a sense of social and environmental stewardship, and do all of this within the hearts and minds of ambitious and well-positioned men and women. It's a bold vision for a graduate school of business.

The contours of human systems

You and I hold bold visions too. We desire to secure deep and lasting transformation in people. We want to leave a true and good legacy, just as do Porkovich, Crener, and their colleagues at the International University of Monaco. We care deeply about making an impact of significance in and through our professions, our institutions, our clients, our communities. In the words of John R. Mott, Nobel laureate and former secretary general of the YMCA, we yearn to "link our lives to a great cause."

Effecting change in human systems is often more difficult than it looks, however. Wherever we each find ourselves right now—at an established organization, an exhilarating start-up venture, a complicated family system, an entrepreneurial initiative, or a personal life of opportunity or of irritation—trying to cause true transformation often feels daunting. Getting a board member, employee, colleague, or client to develop is formidable, sometimes even dangerous. Securing human change, at least change for the good, is tough work, pure and simple.

Developing people, and transforming the human systems that hold people, is like moving an iceberg. The challenge looms on the horizon, massive and mysterious. On our best days, we can imagine the enormous satisfaction of seeing our organizations, professions, or loved ones become solid, buoyant, moving forward, and reaching their full potential. On other days, people and organizations seem destined to wallow in place forever. The optics can mislead us. Change often appears manageable from a distance, maybe even easy from afar, but less so when we draw near. Up close, we realize that we have seen only the tip of the challenge clearly, and below the waterline the rest sinks massively, with contours disappearing into curtains of inky, icy blue.

How do we maneuver a human system so immense? Where do we find the leverage to dislodge and advance it? What about all the parts we can't see, hidden beneath the waterline? And how do we handle the underlying currents that threaten to tug it back toward where we started? These are tough questions for any social enterprise.

Take, for instance, the problem of global obesity. Obesity has become one of the world's most profound and tragic epidemics. Currently, more than 1 billion people can be classified as obese—four times more than merely 25 years ago. Tragically, more than 155 million of these people are children. Today in the United States, the number of adults who are counted as obese is almost one in three. The long-term effects of this epidemic are disastrous; the list of chronic illnesses associated with the disease is staggering. Obesity is not only threatening the quality of life for countless people but simultaneously crippling our health systems. It's a frightful human iceberg in need of turning.

Early in 2000, three bright and ambitious Brits, Harry MacMillan, Paul Sacher, and Dr. Paul Chadwick, joined forces and recruited a team of like-minded activists to a take on the challenge of eradicating obesity. They decided to intervene in the growing epidemic and help people enjoy "fitter, healthier, happier lives." They focused on the underprivileged and underserved, those most at risk for obesity, and founded an organization called MEND Central that is based in the United Kingdom but rapidly expanding worldwide. They are tugging at one of the largest, most intractable icebergs in public health today.

Or, consider the opportunity and challenge of developing healthy communities in a world class, multi-cultural city. Greater Vancouver, British Columbia, is home to more than 2 million people, many of whom are first or second generation immigrants gathered from the vast reaches of the globe and drawn by the promise of peace and prosperity. Vancouver is one of the world's most beautiful cities, bounded by the Pacific Ocean to the west and ridged by ragged, snow-capped mountains to the north and east. It is populated by a skilled, energetic, and diverse population. But the beauty on the surface of any city this size and complexion belies profound needs—poverty, isolation, cultural disconnectedness, social disorientation, and a search of belonging, meaning, and purpose. Communities in Vancouver, as in every other world-class city, need their citizenry to grow and thrive in mind, body, and spirit.

A few years ago the YMCA of Greater Vancouver, which has had a presence of service in the city for 125 years, replaced their old, iconic downtown site with a shining, state-of-the-art complex positioned impressively at the city's epicenter. Since the opening, it's been a magnet for public interest and attention. Simon Adams, the general manager, and his leadership team intend for their new YMCA to be a platform for engaging the community and improving the welfare of the children, families, and individuals in the downtown core of Vancouver. Transforming the social and physical wellness of such a sizeable and diverse population is a major undertaking, however. It's another iceberg to be moved.

Or, take the challenge of restructuring a school district to improve the ways faculty and staff members reach and educate children. In the lower mainland of British Columbia, the administrators of School District 33 are navigating a district-wide reorganization. They are merging three departments into one. Their intent is to coordinate resources and increase cogency of programs so that they can achieve greater impact in the lives of children and families. A shrinking economy and seemingly endless litany of child and family needs are putting a squeeze on their already thinly-stretched resources. They have to find a way to streamline operations, align roles, and refocus faculty and staff to develop one effective and inspired team out of three.

Dr. Ruth Weibe, the associate superintendent in School District 33, and her administrative leaders are tasked with the reengineering. The district serves a complex community in an expansive and largely agricultural region of the southern mainland, a region filled with a dizzying array of cultures and ethnicities from along a wide socio-economic range. In many ways, the school district is the glue that holds the disparate factions of the community together. It's one of the most vital forces for social formation. And it's another iceberg to be moved.

These three—a global epidemic, the wellness of people in a city's core, a school district's faculty and staff—are all examples of human systems with more to them than what meets the eye. There is a tip to each iceberg, clearly: improve eating and exercise habits; increase participation in community-engagement and wellness programs; secure alignment to a district's updated programs and procedures. But actually changing the fundamentals within people so that progress is durable and lasting is a different, deeper matter. It will take more than a simple or superficial push. Our own icebergs will require the same to get moving.

An unseen challenge

When we climb into a role of influence and paddle up to a human system, we usually suspect we are in for a challenge. We imagine it might take the best of our effort to help people grow and develop. Yet as long as we lean into it with sufficient vigor, we assume we will manage some modicum of true change. After all, we are not out to accomplish everything—just *this* change with *these* people. All too often however, despite our honest effort, the human system sits immovable—a leaning block of obdurate ice. The organization won't change. The employee won't grow. The community won't improve. Our staff won't head in the right direction. Our clients won't attain or sustain development.

With any iceberg, as with any human opportunity or social problem, a visible tip protruding from the water's surface belongs to a larger mass of iceberg below. Oceanographers claim that between 85 and 90 percent of a typical iceberg's mass lies under the surface. Similarly, down in the depths of any human system are elusive elements—perceptions, beliefs, values, dispositions, identities, positions, energies, and aspirations. These larger and weightier features, less visible from the surface, anchor our iceberg and keep it from moving. Pushing primarily on actionable, viewable, measurable items above the waterline often fails to leverage transformation in the heart of the human system below the surface. We are left exhausted and frustrated with nothing much to show for our effort.

We have to dive in, but how? How do we engage human systems below the waterline? How do we intervene in the deeper and more fundamental elements of our organizations, our staff members, our communities? How can we unlock underlying pockets of potential and engage those hidden but weighty features of obduracy?

In a moment, we will talk about how to apply leverage below the waterline. Before we do, however, let's consider three pressures that tempt us to keep pushing on the surface: the impulse for the quick win, the allure of the best practice, and the challenge of getting to why.

The impulse for the quick win

Imagine yourself with Boris Porkovich at the International University of Monaco. You have a chance to shape emerging business leaders. You have gathered a group of accomplished scholars to your faculty and recruited some of the brightest and most ambitious students from southern Europe. Your grand vision is to make a difference in the conduct of international business practice. What would you do? How would you proceed?

It would be tempting to seek an immediate *quick win*. It's natural to try something, anything actually, to secure quick and visible progress.

Our instinct might be to call together a committee and ask something like, "We have this wonderful opportunity; what is something we can do right now, our 'low-hanging fruit'?" In no time we would generate ideas:

⋯⟩ Add an elective track in social responsibility to our curriculum.

⋯⟩ Require a class in sustainability and social stewardship for all first-year MBA students.

⋯⟩ Offer an annual symposium on values-based leadership.

These are concrete steps, clear and actionable. We could get moving right away. Someone from our committee secures the venue. Another recruits a renowned lecturer. We are off and running!

Achieving a quick win might serve to encourage us all, and maybe even convince some of the more recalcitrant to join the cause, drawn, as people tend to be, by whatever a crowd happens to be doing. But if these quick wins were our focus, we would likely make little more than a momentary splash. Unless they somehow touched the deeper, more elemental positions—the core beliefs of university students, the mind-set of those living in the Principality of Monaco, the critical default values of the business community—they will probably have little lasting impact.

Consider an approach from the banking sector, the strategy of Muhammad Yunus, Nobel Peace Prize winner in 2006 and founder of the Grameen Bank. The bank is one of the first to explore microcredit as a means for social action, offering loans to the impoverished in Bangladesh and beyond. The bank provides critical but miniscule amounts of funding to the poor, amounts too small to be meaningful on any corporate banking ledger in the developed world—only enough to fund, for example, a sewing machine or a milking goat. But more than the inconceivably modest size of the average loan, the strategy of social engagement at Grameen is unique. The bank negotiates almost exclusively with women. It organizes them in social groups for support and accountability. It gives them a personal experience of entrepreneurship. It situates development in capitalism, not in charity, even though (and perhaps, because) one of the key aims is ongoing social transformation.

In recent years, many micro-lending enterprises have fallen prey to mismanagement and corruption, as often happens when people and money come together in the hands of the unscrupulous. The illustration is still apt, however. Micro-lending holds possibility to engage the social and cultural dimension of the poverty iceberg. It provides loans for the underserved, certainly. But it also has potential to intervene in the underlying issues that cause and perpetuate poverty. More than providing access to capital, its true value is in catalyzing personal agency, social support, and entrepreneurship among women, thereby empowering the culturally powerless. The Grameen Bank reports that 7 million impoverished, of whom 97 percent are women in over 70,000 villages across Bangladesh, currently receive unsecured loans to fund small enterprises. A staggering 58 percent of those— over 3.5 million—have made measurable progress toward escaping the clutches of poverty. Mismanagement in the micro-lending sector notwithstanding, the iceberg of poverty in Bangladesh appears to be on the move.

The genius of Yunus' ideas is in their power to penetrate below the surface and touch the fundamentals of human beliefs—the mind-set, social mores, motivations, pockets of energy, areas of social resistance, and sparks of ambition buried in culture and gender. In contrast, the ideas offered by our imaginary committee at the University of Monaco, if taken at face value, are superficial, overlaying programs on top of a classic MBA. There is nothing wrong with a quick win. We should prefer action over inaction. However, striking before we truly understand the underlying issues within people that cause social irresponsibility in business will inhibit our iceberg-moving efforts. Our committee has yet to identify a good strategy to reconstruct the deeper motivations of people and re-animate the human systems within the business community. Merely adding a course or elective or symposium usually won't do. We might accomplish some good, but most likely because we have gathered attention to the issues and not because we have engineered an iceberg-moving design.

The allure of the best practice

Our attraction to action also leads us to chase the next *best practice*. At first glance, seeking a best practice seems to make sense. Certainly, much can be gained from adopting an industry's exemplary behaviors. Best practices upgrade our performances and help us raise ourselves to our sector's high bar. It would be folly not to learn from the success of others. The problem, however, is that the allure of the best practice often (and ironically) conspires against our iceberg-moving efforts. We err when we assume that if we can just find the latest technique, we will have found the secret to moving the human system. Our hope that people will be transformed through best practice alone is often illusory, and we succumb to any number of key errors:

⋯⟩ **Error of congruence.** We adopt a best practice that is incompatible with or inhospitable to our organizational culture and then, in no time, reject the transplanted practice like a human body rejects the transplant of a mismatched organ.

⋯⟩ **Error of underpinnings.** We take a best practice without examining the underlying precepts that must be held to practice it well, thereby rendering the practice inert.

⋯⟩ **Error of competing emphases.** We add a best practice uncritically to a line-up of rival best practices, diffusing the energy and focus needed to employ the practice effectively while we chase the "latest and greatest."

⋯⟩ **Error of context.** We seek a best practice that worked well in a different context at a different time, but is ill-fitted for our current context and stage of development.

···❯ **Error of satiety.** Most precariously, we adopt best practices to satisfy ourselves with tightening our efficiencies and raising our productivity, and in so doing fool ourselves by assuming that performing better is the same thing as transforming the lives of others.

Adopting an industry best practice might be exactly what we need to discipline ourselves to do better. However, and much too often, a best practice upgrades the appearance above the waterline and does little to move the whole iceberg.

Consider the strategy developed by those at Teach for America. For over two decades, they have been recruiting and training some of the best and brightest college graduates from among the most esteemed universities representing a variety of academic disciplines and commissioning them to teach in the classrooms of troubled and underprivileged communities across the country. They invite fresh college graduates to take two-year stints serving in some of the nation's worst educational environments. To date, more than 3 million children in over 43 regions in the United States have been served by these young teacher-activists. Their organization has been leading an educational revolution in troubled communities across America.

The approach of Teach for America is a break from tradition. To remedy educational inequity, most conventional efforts have tried to reform schools from within. Theirs has infused the profession with help from without. Most efforts have utilized veterans; theirs mobilizes young people right out of college. Most have focused on individual teachers in individual classrooms; theirs gathers a corps and gives them a social experience of collective activism, modeling social movements like the Peace Corps and the American Civil Rights movement. Most efforts have worked within the bounds of the education profession; theirs deliberately gives young graduates from a variety of disciplines a high-dose experience, believing that they will return to their chosen professions and advocate the rest of their lives from platforms spanning our society for educational equity. If they had sought best practices alone, they would have replayed traditional educational reform, only better. Instead, they designed a new and powerful movement of change that, along with developments within professional teaching guilds, is poised to turn the iceberg of educational inequality.

Searching for a best practice can actually distract from the real, difference-making work. It's not just that we fail to innovate. It's that a best practice can take our attention away from diagnosing and intervening in the ideas people hold and the way they hold ideas, thereby imperiling our iceberg-moving mission. A best practice is often at the tip of the iceberg. We need best practices. However, we also need to engage below-the-surface—those core and root elements of human systems—to move the whole iceberg. True change begins with a courageous look at the Why beneath it all, and this is a question we tend to avoid.

The challenge of getting to why

We are much more accustomed to talking about the What ("let me tell you about the program we are running"), the Who ("this is our cast of characters"), and even the How ("here is the process we use"), than the Why. Think about your last staff meeting. What did you talk about most? How much of your meeting was taken up by the What, the Who, and the How? When was the last time your team engaged the Why of it all (not simply the Why as in "what for," but also the Why as in "why are people struggling to grow and develop" and "why are some interventions leveraging true and durable change better than others")? Tactics, timelines, and financial tables are all important to any managerial meeting, no doubt. But if your meetings are like most of ours, they are monopolized by What, Who, and How.

Think about your personal life for a moment. You get up in the morning, and you have a list in your head of things to do. Your schedule is bearing down on you. Time, you know, is a precious and fleeting commodity. As acting manager of your life, you have to fit everything in and get it all done. You have so much to do and not much space to think about the underlying ideology of your day—what you stand for, what you are giving your life to, how your assumptions about yourself and your strategies for life are influencing your choices, how your inner beliefs and bearing are causing you to show up as you do. If you are like most, you have your hands full simply trying to check off your "to do" list. Examining the Why, however, could be personally transformational.

Diving into the Why beneath our What, How, and Who, both corporately and personally, is unnerving. So much of our own identity is wrapped up in what we do. We have a nagging hunch that we need to examine human causality in deeper, more robust ways, but we also suspect it might threaten the status quo. For instance, what if we discovered that root dispositions of humanity (like beliefs, hopes, and fears) were to blame for how things happen to be in our organizations? Changing those might require touching the deeper parts in people, or the deeper parts in our organizations or professions or communities. That wasn't part of the job description when we signed up—meddling with the inner lives of others. Few of us were told that we would need to dive productively into the heads and hearts of people to be successful. Even more troublesome, what if we found areas of complicity hidden in ourselves, implicating ourselves, illuminating resistance within our own mind-set and makeup that sabotage our efforts to influence change in others? Such discoveries would be disquieting, for progress would require the productive disruption and renovation of our own lives.

In addition, we are all so busy. Our work never seems to slow. We have a sense that pausing is inherently destabilizing—just like the lesson we each learned years ago when first trying to gain balance on a bicycle. Do you remember what it was like learning how to ride? You quickly discovered that you had to keep moving forward in order not to fall. Years later, that early lesson is ingrained in our psyches. Many of us pedal furiously at our work so that we don't tip over. Pausing to engage a deeper Why puts at risk the stability that comes from constantly pushing forward.

What if we stopped for a moment to ask a couple of Why questions? What if we allowed the moment to ask us a few in return? Here are some possibilities. Feel free to add your own to our list:

⋯⟩ Why are we here, in this place and at this point in history, giving our lives for this?

⋯⟩ Why are we stuck doing things as we always have, seemingly unable to do them fundamentally better?

⋯⟩ Why is lasting change so difficult to secure in my coworker, my staff member, my organization, my community?

⋯⟩ Why are we only this effective in causing impact, and no more?

⋯⟩ Why can't we shake these problems within our organizational culture?

⋯⟩ Why do the people we serve seem so resistant to change?

⋯⟩ Why is "who we say we are" at such odds with "how we show up"?

⋯⟩ Why is it that what seems most important also feels most unattainable, uncontrollable, and immeasurable?

A Why is a tough question to answer well. It forces us to think about underlying issues, the subtle but powerful meanings embedded in the human system. It makes us explore human leanings, values, beliefs, hopes, dreams, trajectories. Asking Why maneuvers us into deep assumptions, both tacit and explicit. It helps us dig into callous areas of human intractability and feel around tender areas of human vulnerability. It is complex, mysterious, exhilarating. It is work.

When a child asks you, "why this" or "why that," you can simply answer with a What, Who, or How and leave it at that. Those of you who have been around children have discovered this trick by now. Answer a child's Why question with a What, Who, or How and you will have satisfied their itching curiosity. It's a fine tactic when speaking with a young child. However, we tend to do the same in our lives and work. We fill our conversations with What, Who, and How and then distract ourselves with our important, but endless list of activity. It's endemic among us all. The former president of the Czech Republic, Václav Havel, once called our tendency to fixate on tasks a "cult of action." We certainly need a plan of action, but we also need a point of collective reflection. We need a way to think about the Why so that we might know how best to influence the human systems around us.

Beneath the surface

Our big idea so far is this: There are reasons we tend to focus on the surface of human systems—the impulse for the quick win, the allure of the best practice, and our reluctance to think deeply enough about the underlying Why. Yet we know it is not enough to engage people superficially. We have to go below the surface if we are to make progress on challenges above the surface. Intervening on both sides of the waterline is what makes the Grameen Bank and Teach for America gain leverage to move icebergs. It is also what Porkovich and Crener desire to achieve at the International University of Monaco.

Any institution, especially a start-up, is pressed to show a good iceberg's tip. For the International University of Monaco, progress has come quickly. It has only been six years since the university reorganized and repositioned itself, but it has already rocketed to 35 on the *The Economist's* ranking of hundreds of business schools worldwide. For an educational institution, the surface of the iceberg is obvious: student-faculty ratios, program offerings, employment of graduates, faculty publications, among others. These indices, to a great extent, determine rankings, rankings influence the institution's reputation, and reputation ensures the institution's prosperity. It is critical, then, to perform well on visible, above-the-surface markers if you want to distinguish yourself.

Since the International University of Monaco has quickly attained an enviable rank among the worldwide mass of business schools, can you imagine how tempting it might be to rely on the institution's performance review as a proxy for impact? It's hard to argue with ranking. A rank is visible to everyone. It would be easy to seduce ourselves into thinking we were making an impact simply because we had attained high marks in the eyes of evaluators at *The Economist*. We could become so enamored with inching the ranking needle ever higher into the future that we distract ourselves from true difference-making.

It's a typically balmy, early autumn day along the Côte d' Azure. The Mediterranean Sea shimmers pleasantly on one side, and the Principality of Monaco hums with restless energy on the other. I break away from the lectures I am giving as a visiting professor in the doctoral program of business and meet Porkovich and Crener for a mid-afternoon lunch of pasta and wine in a modern Monegasque café around the corner from the university. There, we talk about the future of their institution. They describe how the ranking system pushes them to do well. It benchmarks programs, exposes weaknesses, rewards performance. It compares them to business schools worldwide and rewards their hard work by publishing their status to their readership. They have been diligent to perform well. You can't miss it. It's practically unheard of within higher education to achieve a ranking so high so quickly.

While Porkovich and Crener are both pleased, however, neither is satisfied. It's not that their rank is insufficiently high. It's just that they realize their ranking does little to indicate whether they are achieving the essence of their bold vision. They desire to influence the business mind-set and culture, not just do business school. They don't want to settle for needle-moving; they want to be moving icebergs. This means their effectiveness will be measured by a different, more qualitative gauge of significance. And so our conversation turns to deeper, more qualitative aspirations as we lean forward to hear each other talk amidst the café's din.

This is no different from the challenge we each face. There are forces that fix our attention on the surface. There are pressures we feel to mistake a busy and active organization for an iceberg-moving one. We, too, get seduced into thinking that activity, tidiness, compliance, efficiency, scale, and reputation are the same thing as true and durable human transformation. We know instinctively, however, that it is possible for programs to run well, needles to move, and ranking to be secured, with no true or durable impact made in people.

So how do we proceed toward true human impact? How do we develop effective strategies for moving human systems? How do we form the deeper parts of people and organizations? And how do we intervene when we find vital parts malformed? We need to be able to see what lies below the surface and then engage strategically in what we find.

Let's begin with the task of seeing.

2. Diving In

There is a difference between looking and seeing. Elliot Eisner, a Stanford University professor and pioneer in the practice of qualitative inquiry—a form of research that steps away from a strictly numerical form of measurement and examines the intangibles and subtle but significant qualities of human situations—makes this distinction.

To look, we need only to open our eyes. It's a natural thing to do, to look. We look all the time. We look at ourselves, our colleagues, our organizations, our communities. Looking is relatively easy. It needs no particular depth of insight. It needs no deeper dive.

Seeing, however, is a different matter, especially when we seek to see below the waterline in a human system. To see well, we have to know what to pay attention to. We have to focus on key elements and core qualities and not confuse or distract ourselves with interesting but peripheral human features. We have to interpret and make meaning of what is going on in the human system and come to understand why it is so. Eisner observes, "Looking is a necessary condition, but looking is essentially a task one undertakes; it is seeing that is an achievement."

If we were simply to look at the International University of Monaco, we would quickly spot the indicators of ranking. They bubble up to the surface, clear and obvious. But how would we dive down *into* the International University of Monaco and *into* the milieu of the business community it seeks to affect? If we were to look at the global problem of obesity, or the wellness landscape of Vancouver, or the culture of School District 33, we could note plenty of surface indicators. But how would we dive *into* the human causes of obesity, or into the human conditions that comprise the health of communities in Vancouver, or into the human dynamics that give education power and cogency in School District 33?

Seeing into the depths of any human system—whether an individual, community, or institution—requires us to know where and how to look. But it's easy to get disoriented once we get down into the muck of human systems. People are wonderfully and terribly complex, and groups of people are even more so. There is so much going on under the surface. We need help to explore it all well. We need a reliable apparatus to give us a disciplined and pointed dive so that when we get down into our human systems and look at what is causing them to be as they are, we end up seeing.

How to see

For some time, scholars have wrestled with the challenge of making sense of the murkier and more imponderable parts of human systems. A particularly elegant schema was once proffered by William Frankena, former chair of the philosophy department at the University of Michigan. He suggested that different kinds of ideas drive people and human systems to action. The notion that ideas, and people's commitments to ideas, determine movement and progress (or stubbornness and stasis) is nothing new or revolutionary. What is particularly helpful about his model, however, is the recognition that the ideas can be categorized as unique species (for ease of use, we will call them *boxes* to designate a holding place for types of ideas) and that they come in layers. We are going to build on his ideas, modifying and developing them in the remaining pages. But in order for you to visualize the model and see where we are going, here's what these categories of ideas look like as discrete chunks within our iceberg:

You'll notice immediately that there is one box above the waterline, and two levels of two boxes each below the waterline. We visualize what the tip of the iceberg looks like. Then, we see that there are two types of ideas in the first layer down immediately beneath the tip. And then, there are two additional kinds of ideas even a layer below, way down where the iceberg is most deeply anchored in place. We are lettering these chunks, or boxes, in our iceberg to help us reference them easily.

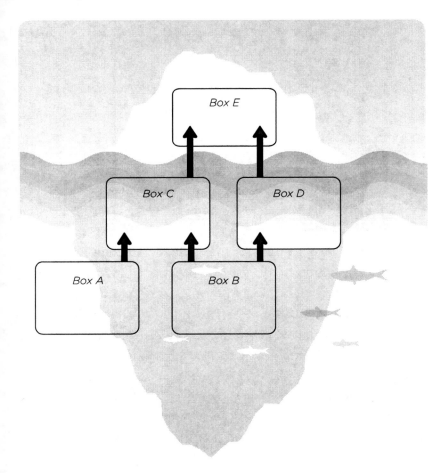

Let's give our iceberg a brief tour.

Box E - Action

On the surface, as we have already noted, is a category we will call Box E – *Action*. It is what you say and do and feel. If you are working out your own personal iceberg, the iceberg of your organization, or the iceberg of those you seek to influence, place everything that is easy to observe in Box E – *Action*. Take a good inventory. These are the obvious parts of human systems.

> *Box E*
> **Action**
> Program, Event, Service, Initiative,
> Behavior, Course, Message, Reaction,
> Words, Performance, Seminar,
> Display of Emotion

If the human system you are working with is an organization, Box E – *Action* most likely contains the programs, initiatives, behaviors, performance, relationships, and various other organizational expressions and outputs. If you are working with a community, Box E – *Action* is the philanthropic activity, health behavior, crime statistics, high school graduation rates, community volunteerism, economic investments, and similar indicators of collective action within a community. If you are thinking about yourself and a personal iceberg, your Box E – *Action* is filled with meetings, calls, appointments, and tasks on your daily schedule. It is also what you do and say and feel that is not exactly in your day-planner but shows up throughout your day nonetheless. If someone were to follow you around with a video recorder today, capturing your every word and deed, your Box E – *Action* is what they would see.

For a moment, think about the Box E – *Action* of the icebergs in front of the leaders at MEND, the YMCA of Greater Vancouver, and School District 33. If it is what a person says, feels, and does, then Box E—*Action* is a child choosing a healthy snack, a resident stepping up to volunteer for the first time, a teacher inviting a school counselor to help develop a classroom's atmosphere of learning. It is also what a collection of people say, feel, and do—the changing statistics in Body Mass Index (BMI) of kids in the United Kingdom, the trajectories of philanthropic activity throughout Vancouver, and the culture of collaboration within the school district in Chilliwack. Box E—*Action* is the visible surface of the human system, the parts we see and hear every day.

But action, we know, is only the tip of the iceberg.

The first layer down

We are going to dive in now, and these ideas might change how you think about the human systems you are a part of as well as those you are seeking to move. As we begin to explore below the waterline, remember that these principles apply to any human system—an individual, family, organization, profession, community, nation. Also, keep in mind that we are looking in order to be able to see. What we actually see is a different matter. In other words, you might find that below the waterline, the human system is robust and well-developed, or full of malformations and open cavities. You might not think there is much below there, and you could be right. Or, there may be commitments and positions that are formed improperly and, apart from significant re-shaping, will keep the iceberg anchored to this place forever. In any case, we need to know what to look for.

Beneath Box E – *Action,* one layer down in the water but close to the surface, are two kinds of ideas that most directly affect action.

Box C - *Intended Impact*

Consider, for a moment, why we act as we do. We usually want something—we want to achieve something, accomplish something, avoid something, or secure something. On our most intention-filled days, we want to impact something in someone else. Box C – *Intended Impact* is just that: intention about impact.

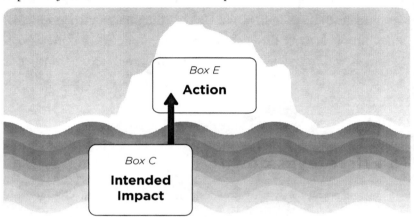

A Box C – *Intended Impact* is a driving force, and a stabilizing one. It keeps our action engaged and purposeful instead of haphazard and endlessly busy. It also keeps our eyes fixed on how the world will be different because we have been here. I was leading a workshop on strategy the other day with a group of bright and gifted managers, and they continually wanted to talk about the services they provided instead of the end to which those services were designed. We kept having to ask, "To what end?" and "In service to what?" to stay focused on impact. Box C makes us think about what we intend to influence in others.

A solid Box C – *Intended Impact* defines the difference we seek to make in the lives of those we serve. Box C holds our ideas of human, social, and community effect. For example, this might be the kind of citizenship we desire to achieve among a neighborhood's residents, or a sense of purpose, meaning, and engagement among an institution's employees, or confidence and agency we want our youth to exhibit. Box C—*Intended Impact* identifies the changes in others and our world that we intend to cause.

As you might imagine, sometimes we don't think very carefully about our intention. Sometimes we do things simply because they are the easiest things to do, or because we have always done them this way, or because everyone else seems to be doing similarly. This results in an under-development of Box C – *Intended Impact,* a cavity in the core of our iceberg that makes us both shallow (personally or organizationally) and unstable (allowing us to be blown and tossed by wind and waves of the day).

Developing a good Box C – *Intended Impact* pushes us to think about others, and this is often challenging for us. We tend to want to write goals for ourselves (like, "to be the organization people go to first," or "to double the size of our offerings") instead of what we intend to impact in others (like, "resiliency among at-risk youth," or "a sense of belonging among the marginalized in this community"). But without a clear and well-developed Box C – *Intended Impact,* we might simply count all of the things we do (Box E – *Action*) and then declare we have made a difference (Box C – *Intended Impact*). We might mistake our own performance for a vital and durable change in the people we are dedicated to serve.

Notice how the arrow is directed from Box C – *Intended Impact* toward Box E – *Action*. This shows how our actions should depend on our intended impact, and not the other way around. An organization needs first to define the difference it intends to make, the legacy in the world it seeks to leave, and then design and align actions accordingly. Occasionally we confuse the directions of intentionality and find ourselves in missional drift, full of activity but making less of a dent on our world than we would like to imagine. In fact, we can occupy ourselves with a whole host of exceptional activities and see surprisingly little evidence of deep and durable impact in people other than fatigue. Box E often overpowers Box C and tips the iceberg precariously. A mission-driven or cause-driven organization or individual shapes action by the intended impact and holds tightly to a robust Box C – *Intended Impact* at its core.

Here is an example of a couple high-level Box C ideas from the administration of School District 33:

> *Box C for SD33*
> **Intended Impact**
> All we do is in service to developing:
> • Passionate learners who participate and shape their own learning and unique potential.
> • Empowered students who become responsible, caring, and competent citizens.
> • Collective commitments within the school and community to recognize, understand, and embrace diverse success.

Take a moment and think about your ideas of Box C – *Intended Impact.* What is your Box C—*Intended Impact* for yourself, your leadership team, your department or your organization? Are your ideas clear and compelling, and do they determine the choices you make about action? Jot a few of them down on paper and see how they take shape in your mind.

Sometimes our iceberg-strategy stops with Boxes C and E. These are, of course, the essential foundations for any logic model: the connection between what you are doing and what you intend to accomplish. Our schema, however, presents additional categories, groups of ideas often overlooked when examining human systems. These next three boxes are extraordinarily powerful for human change and determine, to a great extent, the leverage we can exert on our systems. Let's get into them.

Box D - *Best Means*

On the same level of Box C – *Intended Impact*, right below the surface, is a set of ideas we will call Box D – *Best Means*. Best means are what we believe should characterize our every action to maximize our intended effect. They are the kinds of methods and strategies we are committed to. They are the principles undergirding our theory of change. For many, theories of change look quite tactical, a simply a break-down of the steps from Box E – *Action* to Box C – *Intended Impact*. The principles of a theory of change, however, are more powerful than the steps or tactics. How do people best grow? How do organizations best develop? How do problems best get solved? What are the keys to human change? These ideas represent our Box D – *Best Means*.

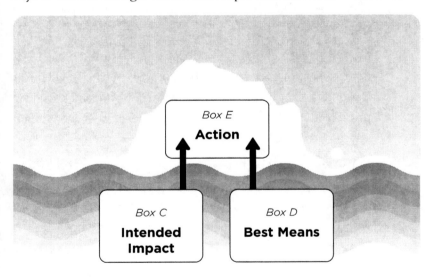

Notice a couple things about Box D – *Best Means:* (1) Box D should hold *principles,* not practices—not even best practices. This is not what we do per se. (Remember, what we do is Box E — *Action.*) Rather, it is why we do this particular action and not another. It is the characteristic of the practice that makes the best practice work so well. (2) Box

D also defines our choices about best means, not simply the means we are using most often. Box D, then, makes us to think about the most transformational features of our actions, initiatives, behaviors, and programs, the DNA of growth and development. It makes us decide which values of process and method best inform the actual tactics we adopt. These are the qualities and characteristics that give our theories of change the power to turn icebergs.

A good Box D – *Best Means* is an extraordinarily helpful set of ideas to develop and apply. Think about some of the implications:

···> **Innovating.** Sometimes we define ourselves by what we do, or what we have always done (Box E); with Box D we are free to design new initiatives that are consistent with our values of change and true to our identity without being stuck in the past.

···> **Modeling.** Sometimes we train people to mimic our way of doing tasks, or the way of a best practice (Box E); with Box D we can teach people to model instead of mimic, to glean principles and apply them in new and fresh ways, fitting their unique personality and context.

···> **Multiplying.** Sometimes we try to extend our reach of influence by replicating or exporting a program (Box E), diluting its power over time as it gets further from the original design; with Box D we can articulate the values and principles underlying the program to help people adopt the "why" not just the "what" and then create iterations for themselves even better than the original.

···> **Onboarding.** Sometimes we bring people into our culture but simply telling them what to do (Box E); with Box D we can help them think and engage more sufficiently and embrace our meaning and ethos.

There are more implications, which we will talk about later, but these are a few examples of how a Box D – *Best Means* works alongside Box C – *Intended Impact* to give substance and shape to the iceberg under the surface. I have seen some leaders become so articulate about their Box D that they need to give only the bare minimum of instruction for Box E – *Action*; their team members thoroughly know how to design and evaluate actions based on their Box D – *Best Means*. And I have witnessed other leaders, with under-developed Box D – *Best Means*, needing to write manual after manual for Box E – *Action* to cover every possible scenario and spell out every possible action for their staff members.

Here are a few examples from a Box D of the Robert Lee YMCA:

Box D for Robert Lee YMCA

Best Means

All we do is characterize by:

- **Meaningful experiences.** People grow best through experiences that inspire them.
- **Intentional relationships and partnerships.** Communities develop best when people experience purposeful, meaningful, relational investments from multiple people and partners.
- **Excellence.** People are drawn best by experiences of quality that evoke the best from them in response.
- **Personal invitations.** People are most likely to become involved when asked.
- **Reflection.** Personal change happens best when we dedicate time to meaningful and guided reflection.
- **Modeling.** People grow best when they see growth modeled for them, when they watch us seek to live according to our core values and ideals every day.

Try it out for yourself. What's your Box D—*Best Means*? What are the principles underlying your theory of change? If you were to identify the key ideas that characterize your personal or professional best means, what would you say? Take a moment and try articulating a few items in your Box D and see what you think about them.

A second layer down

Already, we have more ideas of substance than is often considered in human systems. For instance, why do you do what you doing today? You probably have a to-do list in your head right now, and there is probably predictable ways in which you will handle the tasks and interact with the people represented on that list. But what causes you to walk through your day as you will?

If we were to get into your iceberg and see your personal human system, we would look for your Box C – *Intended Impact* (what kind of impact for others motivates you) as well as your personal Box D – *Best Means* (what kinds of strategies you have adopted to engage tasks and people). If you are like most of us, you might not have a very well-formed Box C or D from which your actions are taking shape. You might just be doing what you have always done, or going through the motions, or trying simply to stay afloat without much thought to your own iceberg-strategy. Our organizations are like that too. We tend to fill ourselves with Box E—*Action* without giving much thought to the substance below the waterline.

One of the main reasons why our ideas of intended impact and best means are under-developed is because we haven't given much attention to the sets of ideas informing and nourishing them. Boxes C and D don't stand in isolation. There is another layer below, a potent and influential layer that forms them. The ideas from the lower tier are the foundation for the iceberg and provide the most substantial source of buoyancy and ballast for our human systems. This layer determines where we are as a human system, how we look as a human system, how we move as a human system, and what kind of leverage we can exert on other human systems around us.

Box B - *Premises*

Consider what informs our ideas of intended impact and best means. What makes us care about having an effect on others or our world? And what makes us value certain means of engagement over others? These don't just appear out of nowhere, they come from somewhere deep within us. They are products of our beliefs. We will represent these beliefs as Box B – *Premises*.

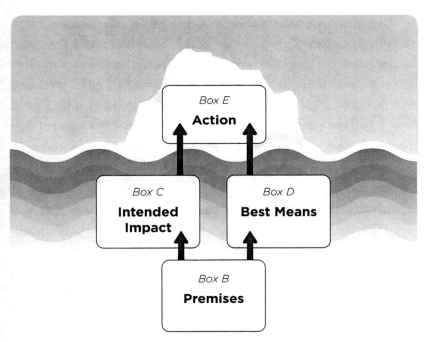

Box B – *Premises* is the part of our human systems that holds our most potent perspectives and convictions. As you might imagine, these core beliefs, even though they are deep within the iceberg, influence everything. They allow us to embrace an intended impact and adopt a best means, or they keep us from authentically becoming who we say we want to be. They can work for us to make our actions brilliant, or against us to undermine our best efforts.

I'm sure you've seen two people occupy the same Box E – *Action* but be worlds apart in influence. They may espouse the same Box C – *Intended Impact* and claim the same Box D – *Best Means*. But if they hold different Box B – *Premises*, their effect is wholly different. They may be doing the same exact action, but animated by a different set of premises. Those underlying premises, in time, make a monumental difference, either filling the action with meaning and verve or overpowering (and sometimes undoing) even the best training people have received in tactics.

One of my associates likes to show groups she is facilitating a copy of her organization's membership policy, and then ask if the group can ascertain the unspoken premises that work their way up through the iceberg and come to light in policy forms. It's quite revealing. As I talk with leaders who are asking for help to develop leadership capacity, or evaluate social impact, or assess corporate culture, I find the beliefs represented in those conversations quite revealing as well. Our deep perceptions and beliefs about ourselves, others, our organizational context, and our world infuse everything about us. Premises are unmistakable once you start paying attention to them. Can you imagine what unspoken premises might be underlying your organizational policies or conversations?

As we seek to develop Box B – *Premises,* we need to think in terms of two types of beliefs: (1) beliefs about context, and (2) beliefs about core convictions. Premises of context (type 1) are our perceptions about the people and the world around us. They are our assumptions about how things work and who we are working with. As you might imagine, our perceptions of context can either be spot-on, helping us design wise and discerning interventions, or skewed by the refractive optics of our own autobiographies, causing us to mishandle people and situations. Core convictions (type 2) are the beliefs we cling to in every context, even in the face of appearances to the contrary. Both kinds of premises work their way through the iceberg of our human systems, individually and collectively.

One of the peculiar characteristics of core convictions is that over time we tend to collect an incongruous set, adopting them *a la carte* as we walk through our lives, often in response to particularly difficult and formative circumstances. Some core convictions we know and herald (like, "We believe all people are worthy," or "To be human is to experience belonging in a relational community"). Other core convictions sneak in unannounced during times of heightened pressure and take root in our collective mind-set (like, "We have to look the best, no matter what the cost," or "If I do not feel needed, I have no value"). The latter can undo us. That is why we will need to give particular attention to our own core convictions and the core convictions of those we seek to influence.

Box B for MEND
Premises of *Core Convictions*

- We believe that people can and need to take personal responsibility for their health.
- We believe that blame is unhelpful.
- We believe in the value of practical action.
- As a social enterprise we believe that we can both do good and do well.

Think about your own human system for a moment. What are your Box B—*Premises*? What have you come to believe about your context and the context of the people around you? To what beliefs are you dedicated? What convictions, intentional or not, drive everything you do? How sufficient are your premises to help you shoulder the vision to which you are called?

Box A - *Ultimate Aims*

We now come to perhaps the most elusive, but also most profound and exciting part of the iceberg. It is at the same depth as Box B – Premises, and both informs and is informed by Box B. It has the potential for being the most stable and sufficient force in our system, but also is the most challenging to maintain with health and vitality and consistency. It is our fountainhead of motive, the place from which all else in our human systems springs. It is our essence, our Box A – *Ultimate Aims*.

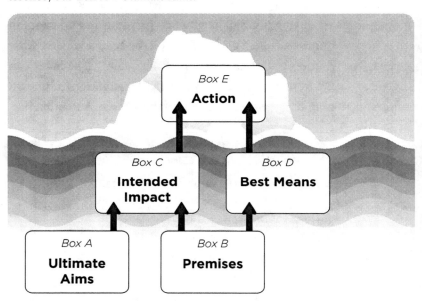

Any human system, regardless of what it believes, is motivated by a prime commitment. This commitment determines how we will "show up" in all things. It is what we ultimately desire to *be* regardless of what we happen to *effect* in every situation. It is the presence we bring to any circumstance, the way we carry ourselves regardless of the circumstance. Box A—*Ultimate Aims* is the power, for good or ill, behind our voice, behind our intent, behind our action. What resides in Box A—*Ultimate Aims* has incalculable consequence, for it is the color and tenor and taste of all our work.

If you are not quite sure what inhabits your Box A, think about what might follow the phrase, "In all things, we will...." No matter how clients treat us, how the economy presses us, or what happens in the politics of our office among colleagues and friends, our Box A – *Ultimate Aims* is what we intend to embody in all things, through any and all circumstances. It reminds us that "we cannot tell others to act responsibly without first being responsible," "we cannot develop charity in others without first being charitable ourselves," "we cannot ask others to give of their best without offering our own full commitment, regardless of how people respond to us." When we nurture a collective Box A—*Ultimate Aims* into a living pulse, healthy and robust, it will unleash a cascade of collective energy and influence.

Sometimes we suppose everything in our human system should flow from mission, from our Box C – *Intended Impact*. But consider that prior to mission, an organization has to be a certain way to carry a mission well. This sense of being is a necessary pre-condition to achievement. When an organizational essence (Box A) aligns with an organizational mission (Box C), the message rings clear and convincing, authentic and true. Without being intentional about what deeply drives us, we run the risk of compromising or even corrupting our best laid plans with an incongruent or, in some cases, toxic presence.

To clarify the difference between A and C: Box A—*Ultimate Aims* is who we intend to be; Box C—*Intended Impact* is what we want to accomplish. Box A is the essence of how we carry ourselves to steward well our mission; Box C is the outcome we would like to achieve in others. We nurture Box A—*Ultimate Aims* in order to achieve Box C—*Intended Impact*. It is critical work to develop Box A. There is probably no such thing as an empty Box A anyway. We all live for something, both individually and collectively. If we don't make decisions about our ultimate aims, they will develop inadvertently and unintentionally in the hearts and minds of everyone involved.

Here is an example of a few ideas of an articulated Box A – *Ultimate Aims* from each of our cases:

Box A
Ultimate Aims

Robert Lee YMCA

In all things we will act with integrity and intentionality. In service to each other and the community, we will in all things embody the YMCA core values of caring, respect, honesty, and responsibility.

MEND

In all things we put health at the heart
In all things we celebrate innovation and partnership
In all things we champion practical action
In all things we act responsibly

School District 33

As passionate learners, in all things we will maintain hope and integrity while honouring all people.

I have found that my personal Box A – *Ultimate Aims,* which is my core motive and should be my most stable sense of self, tends to be less consistent than I would like for it to be. One moment it seems healthy and vital, giving me presence and poise, and the next moment it is corrupted by desires which might be fine in themselves, but which make terrible Box A aspirations. Sometimes when I go to speak to a group of managers, for instance, I realize that I want most to be liked, or to look impressive, or to be seen as smart, or just to cover material, or to get people working—and that as a source of deepest longing and desire in the moment. And then I have to talk to my own heart to get my prime motive squared away and in a better place. For me, it takes constant vigilance and practice to live a good Box A. I think it does for most people and organizations as well.

What is your Box A—*Ultimate Aims*? How do you and your colleagues show up in all things to others? How do you want to show up in all things to others? What might be in your Box A space that shouldn't be there? Where might there be conflicts within your Box A?

Putting it all together in our iceberg metaphor, Box E is the tip protruding from the waterline. As we peer down, we see Boxes C and D, submerged but close to the surface. Below those, deeper and even more fundamental, are Boxes A and B, the iceberg's most significant source of buoyancy, stability, and substance.

We will explore the formative power of these ideas more fully in the next section, but consider for a moment a few brief implications of the model:

⋯> Focusing on Box E – *Action*, and neglecting the other boxes, makes us individually and organizationally shallow and superficial, filled with busyness but lacking substance, depth, and purpose.

⋯> Trying to move people or human systems by managing their Box E – *Action* alone is an exercise in futility; there is far too much below the surface, anchoring the human system in place. The iceberg might temporarily tip forward with an external pull, but will eventually shift back into place once the pressure is lifted.

⋯> Neglecting Box A – *Ultimate Aims* and Box B – *Premises* makes our human systems most precarious. Missing any box of ideas, in fact, leaves a gaping hole.

⋯> Holding ideas in the right place within the iceberg matters. For instance, a powerful idea in Box C – *Intended Impact* is a dangerous and deleterious idea in Box A – *Ultimate Aims*. A great Box D – *Best Means* makes a poor Box C – *Intended Impact*. How we hold ideas, not just what ideas we hold, can make all the difference.

⋯> If we aim to move the icebergs around us, it stands to reason that we need have given attention to the icebergs of ourselves and our own organizations.

We now have two essential tasks before us. To lead people to lasting change, we must (1) develop our own under-the-surface boxes and (2) find a way to influence the under-the-surface boxes of others. In other words, we have to deepen and develop our own ideology so thoroughly that it animates all of our action, and then influence the ideology of those human systems we care about moving.

Garrett Boone, the founder and former CEO of the Container Store, is speaking at a conference in the posh W Hotel in Dallas. I am presenting a workshop down the hall. Eager to hear his thoughts on leadership, I sneak into the back row of the ballroom to listen. Boone is a clear-spoken man, earnest yet reserved, with little flair but loads of substance. His speech is measured, but his message is mesmerizing. He describes how important it is for a whole organization to have a collective, animated, and abiding ideology.

The founders of the Container Store, he explains, pledged early in the life of the company to talk with every employee about the company's philosophy in depth and with transparency. As he tells it, having intentional dialogue about the guiding precepts is a key part of their strategy to give distinction to their company and set it apart from others. I have never been to a Container Store, so I decide to find one and see if I will notice the difference he describes.

For me, it's difficult to imagine a cause less glamorous than selling objects to hold other objects. (It's not the first time I wonder if I am missing the gene for organization.) But walking through the doors, I sense meaning in the air, something that every employee is breathing, something much more than one might expect from a seemingly dull or pedestrian business of object-organizing. Employees on the floor strike me as earnest, thoughtful, and (this may be odd to say about container-selling) passionate. I chat with sales associates and feel like I am touching the fringe of some grand mission to improve human existence through organizing things, a social movement for bringing order to disorder, a noble battle against the contagion of clutter. Their motto is "Who says a store can't change your life?" The employees have tapped into it, and it appears to have captured them.

I catch Boone on the phone one day as he was driving down a central Texas highway. Over the rush-hour din, he explains how every organization needs to hold bold conversations about values and beliefs, purpose and meaning. He and the other founders of the Container Store foster a culture where everyone, at all levels and not just among senior leaders, talks about philosophical issues. They run bi-annual conferences to encourage such reflection, where employees converge on their Coppell, Texas headquarters to engage with senior leaders about company philosophy. It's not simply a talk about tactics; it's an intentional interaction about beliefs and values and guiding ideas. It's about the material under the surface. Their management must feel an enormous temptation, like all of us do, to design a training program for the alignment of behavior (Box E—*Action*) and leave it at that. Instead, they dive in together (Boxes A, B, C, and D), with everyone on their staff.

Beyond the first blush of "this work is fun," people who pour their lives into any good cause need to connect deeply on a Why level. The deeper the connection to the Why, the more capacity will flow toward the What. The tactics of Box E—*Action* may start the connection, but people need more to adhere well, with engagement and passion. A craftsman working joinery with a new piece of furniture increases the surface area for each joint by cutting tongues and grooves. The greater the interlocking surface, the greater the certainty that the joint will hold together. A good joint has to have an ample connected surface for the chair or table or chest of drawers to hold together and function well over time and under pressure. The calculus of attachment dictates that good joints pack a lot of surface into a small space. It works the same way with people. Engaging people in the ideas of Boxes A, B, C, and D amplifies the surface area of connection for everyone involved, from the board of directors to the front-line staff and even among those we serve. This is the calculus of human engagement as well.

The pressure to manage Box E—*Action* solely, however, is bearing down on us constantly. We perform and produce—it's what we are all about. We execute and measure our output—it's what we focus on. It's tough to nurture ideological strength beneath the surface, beneath the immediate and visible, beneath calendars and deadlines and to-do lists. And yet, the substance of our ideology makes our activity meaningful, durable, and effective for others. To return to our iceberg metaphor, when the substance below the surface erodes, the above-the-surface substance sinks. A substantial collective ideology is required to keep buoyant and poised to make an impact in others.

Developing a robust and buoyant ideology for ourselves or our organizations takes more than simply writing ideas correctly in the boxes. In Part II, we will wrestle with how to think well about each of the boxes, and how to develop ourselves and others with our ideas. Getting our own iceberg moving is one thing; moving the icebergs of others is quite another. How do we cause lasting change in other human systems? Let's think more deeply about this challenge and opportunity.

PART 2

DEVELOPING IDEAS
WITHIN PEOPLE

3. Ultimate Aims: Box A

I n Chicago during late September of 1982, when the swelter of summer still clung to the air and a city sped about its early autumn activity, seven people fell ill suddenly and died. Each had unwittingly swallowed a capsule of Extra-Strength Tylenol surreptitiously laced with cyanide.

Within hours of the first death, a Chicago news reporter phoned James Burke, the chairman of Tylenol's Johnson & Johnson, to tell him what was happening. Burke quickly convened a crisis team of seven and instructed them to answer two questions, and to answer them in a particular order: (1) "How do we protect the people?" and (2) "How do we save this product?

News of the unfolding calamity quickly hit the airwaves. A flash of rumors, half-truths, and exaggerations spread like wildfire as a distraught public panicked over the news. Store managers rushed to yank the drug from their shelves. Thousands who had taken a Tylenol that day furtively searched their mirrors for signs of an extra flush of peril. Others pressed their hands to the foreheads of loved ones, feeling to make sure the pills they had offered to ease a headache or fever were doing a good instead of poisonous work.

Managers at Johnson & Johnson were understandably alarmed, both for the welfare of their customers and the future of their company.

Not only did Tylenol account for 17 percent of their total business, but Johnson & Johnson's entire enterprise—from pain medication to baby care—hinged on the trust of their customers. Worried shareholders watched as their company's stock price plunged and market value plummeted $1 billion. How could their company, so dependent on public confidence, recover from such a public disaster?

What followed is quite literally a textbook case in how to handle a public crisis.

Executives at Johnson & Johnson addressed their frantic customers with forthrightness unprecedented at that time. With an extraordinary degree of candor, they stepped straight into the glare of public scrutiny and offered a clear view of all they knew. They did not minimize, deny or defend, distract or deflect. Instead, even in the midst of the unfolding calamity, they talked frankly and with transparency, pledging to earn back the public's trust. As a first step, Burke and his executives, ignoring the advice of consultants and government agents, moved to recall 31 million bottles of Tylenol capsules from store shelves at an estimated cost of $50 million, a major expense in 1982 dollars. It was openness and action on a new level – a brave and bold strategy.

Within two months of the Tylenol deaths, Johnson & Johnson's stock price was rebounding. In five months, the drug regained an astonishing 70 percent of its former market share. Given the magnitude of the consequence and the specter of enduring public wariness, the recovery was remarkably swift and sure. Their strategy had worked.

In retrospect, most experts credit the company's brilliant public relations and the executives' candid responses for restoring the faith of their customers. Johnson & Johnson had quickly alerted news outlets and told consumers temporarily to avoid all Tylenol products. Within the first week they had established two toll-free crisis hotlines, one for concerned consumers and another to update news organizations. Even now, 30 years later, the case is taught in business schools as the quintessential example of how to meet the media during a crisis. At the time, their candor broke sharply from the conventions of corporate parsimony and demonstrated remarkable prescience for handling public opinion with openness. They flawlessly executed a savvy media and public relations plan.

Others argue that Johnson & Johnson's actions spoke louder than their words. They fulfilled their pledges at considerable expense, both immediately and through the ensuing years. They recalled one of their signature drugs nationwide and tightened security procedures on their manufacturing processes. They eventually developed tamper-evident technology, an innovation that would become an industry-leading best practice and later a government-mandated requirement for drug manufacturers. Johnson & Johnson found opportunity in the midst of the crisis to become an industry leader in safety and trustworthiness, making Tylenol a trusted and profitable brand worldwide.

Could it be, however, that neither the tactics of their public relations campaign nor the striking executions of their recovery plan fully explain their success? Could a deeper, more fundamental posture be the true source of their corporate buoyancy?

Do you remember Burke's initial questions for his team? Notice again the order in which he asked them:

1. "How do we protect the people?"
2. "How do we save this product?"

The sequence of his initial questions reveals an underlying prioritization of values and motivations—a Box A—*Ultimate Aims*. First, protect people. Second, save the product. This is in contrast to much of what we experience in our organizations regardless of whether we belong to for-profit or not-for-profit enterprises. We tend to consider our own interests and livelihoods, positions, and reputations first. But not Johnson & Johnson. Not in this instance. Under such pressure, how did they manage to stay rightly oriented to their first aim?

At a meeting two years prior, the board of directors set out to prioritize responsibilities and articulate their most fundamental commitments. When they emerged from the boardroom, this is what they wrote: "We believe our first responsibility is to the doctors, nurses and patients, to mothers, and all others who use our products and services." (In 1987, the word "fathers" was added.) That's how the executives at Johnson & Johnson came to be driven by a common commitment first and foremost to the welfare of the people they served, even if this commitment appeared temporarily to be at odds with protecting their reputation.

For a moment, think about what was outside the bounds of their control. No matter how brilliant their intervention, they could neither guarantee an empathetic view from news reporters nor ultimately control what their customers thought and did. What was in their control however, was their own driving motive and their company's primary commitment. This was absolutely within their sphere of sovereignty. Staying faithful to this Box A—*Ultimate Aims* guided them, protected them, and ushered them back into the public's good graces.

Sometimes we expect that if we can just find the right technique and execute it flawlessly, we will have in our possession the sole key to success. But no technique can compensate for a poor ultimate aim simply because no good tactic can overpower a bad essence. A good plan, performed with the wrong motive and filled with the wrong kind of energy, will ultimately flounder. Action is best animated by authenticity, not expediency. A public relations firm can spin the words of a CEO during a crisis, but over time the true essence of ultimate motive will seep through and its aroma will be evident to all. Just ask the executives of British Petroleum after the fouling of the Gulf of Mexico in April, 2010, how savvy the public is at sniffing out deep organizational motives. This aroma is what we are calling Box A—*Ultimate Aims*.

Box A—*Ultimate Aims* is useful for more than averting crisis, of course, even though crises tend to expose our ultimate aims most clearly. Every action, interaction, initiative, and strategy is animated by an ultimate aim. Finding a way to form sufficient ultimate aims—nurturing the integration of our personal and our professional Box A, overhauling malformed or inadequately developed Box A, holding ourselves personally and collectively to our ideal Box A, helping to shape and nurture the Box As of those we serve—is essential to causing deep and durable change. It is the single most significant point of leverage for moving the iceberg of our human systems.

The essence of an ultimate aim

Essentially, Box A—*Ultimate Aims* is about who we are—our character, our core, our attitude, our essence. It is our source of motive, center of value, and commitment of being. It is our organizational heart. Regardless of what we might be achieving or how others happen to be responding, and regardless of whether our circumstances are exhilarating or depressing, Box A is how we "show up" in the moment, and how we are committed to "show up" in all future moments.

Most naturally, we think of Ultimate Aims as our mission, but mission is more accurately Box C—*Intended Impact.* Box A—*Ultimate Aims* actually precedes mission. It undergirds mission. It animates mission. To conceive Box A well, it might be helpful for us to re-orient our perspectives in two ways:

1. Ultimate aims are who we are in all things

One way to think about Box A—*Ultimate Aims* is to consider how we might finish a sentence starting, "In all things we will be...." *In all things* we will be respectful, even with those who don't treat us with respect. *In all things* we will be authentic, living the values that we hope to instill in others. *In all things* we will be bringing the best of ourselves, even when no one is looking and our best goes unnoticed. In all things we will be hopeful and persevering, even when those we lead appear entrenched, recalcitrant, or resistant.

Take, for example, the recent rebranding efforts of the YMCAs in the United States, a federation of organizations that collectively represents one of the largest nonprofit efforts in the U.S. YMCAs across the country are adopting a set of ideas called the "voice of the brand." It is the way they want their brand, and their every interaction in the community, to be experienced. Their voice, they have determined, should be genuine, nurturing, welcoming, determined, and hopeful *in all things*. This will be their Box A—*Ultimate Aims* if it is held in a Box A space and if it truly animates their every effort.

Or, consider the consultants of Coraggio Group Inc., a boutique consulting group based in Portland, Oregon that helps companies develop strategy and negotiate organizational change. They have proposed a set of fundamentals—courage, grace, truth, and humility—that they want to characterize their every engagement. *In all things* they intend to exhibit courage, grace, truth, and humility. Coraggio consultants enter human systems at the sharp point of strategy, the place in organizations where mission, personal agenda, capacity, organizational culture, and context converge. They are diving into murky human systems. How can they keep a clear head to intervene wisely and incisively amidst a vortex of disorienting pressures? We can imagine how important it is for them to be both courageous *and* graceful, to be both truthful *and* humble *in all things*, and to exhibit each fully and none at the expense of another.

2. Ultimate aims are our primary source of meaning

Another way to think about Box A—*Ultimate Aims* is to consider what constitutes our ultimate sense of meaning. Determining personal and collective meaning is no small task. Victor Frankl, a holocaust survivor, wrote persuasively after emerging from the horror of a Nazi prison-camp experience, "Man's search for meaning is the primary motivation of his life and not a 'secondary rationalization' of instinctual drives." Discovering our source of meaning gives us a sense of

who we are, both individually and collectively, and who we would like
to be. It is the signature of Box A—*Ultimate Aims*.

Most of us, when we contemplate meaning, tend to think about
mission. We conflate the reason we are giving our lives for the cause
with what we hope to achieve through the cause. Mission is clearly a
driving motivator, but there is also meaning *prior* to mission. There is a
source of motivation that *precedes* what we intend to accomplish. Consider this: What causes you to care about the mission? What makes
you the kind of people or organization that can shoulder your mission
well? By what standard will you evaluate ourselves if, at some point,
you found progress on your mission blocked? Here, in your meaning
of essence, a layer below your meaning of mission, is where we find
Box A—*Ultimate Aims*.

We sometimes avoid talking about meaning within our organizations because we assume that it's best left to private reflection, that
getting people to think about their deeper source of motivation is too
personal or invasive for corporate conversation. But if Frankl is right,
if meaning is the "primary motivation" of every human being, then no
organization seeking to rally the passion of people, engage employees,
or win the hearts and minds of a community can afford to neglect Box
A—*Ultimate Aims*.

If the quest for meaning is a primary human motivation, even the
primary source of motivation, then it will surface regardless of our
attention. It will make its presence felt wherever humans gather, for
no human system can avoid meaning-making. We can either be deliberate about its development or it will form unintentionally. In other
words, we can't choose not to have a Box A—Ultimate Aims; we can
only choose to have it either examined or unexamined, congruent or
incongruous, robust or malformed and underdeveloped, meaningful
or void of meaning, common or disparate. This is why we often find
ourselves joined with others in a common mission (Box C) to follow
a common and carefully aligned work plan (Box E) only to discover

people showing up in surprisingly different ways. We might have superficial alignment but deeper incompatibility for lack of a common or sufficient Box A—*Ultimate Aims*.

Years ago, during the long summer days of my childhood I remember my mother making pickles from the baskets of cucumbers my brothers and I would bring in from our vegetable garden down the street. I don't recall exactly how she did it; to this day it's a great mystery to me. I do remember smelling pickle concoctions boil on the stovetop hour after hour and late into the evening. She packed sliced cucumbers into wide-mouthed glass jars filled with pickle juice and stacked them in neat rows along shelves in her food pantry. Over time, the sweet brine seeped mysteriously and invariably through the vegetables, turning them into pickles.

Such is the power of the substance that permeates the object—the potential to change that object's very identity. A cucumber becomes a pickle. An organization becomes its Box A—*Ultimate Aims*. Everything dropped into the mix bears the unmistakable aroma and is unmistakably changed. A neglected Box A—*Ultimate Aims* will produce an unsavory aroma. An intentional and coherent Box A — *Ultimate Aims* will hold extraordinary power for permeating a human system and transforming it from what it currently is to what it ultimately needs to be.

FORMING A BOX A

For a Box A—*Ultimate Aims* to be powerful and transformational, it should exhibit three characteristics: (1) immediate—accessible in the present, (2) sovereign—within our control, regardless of the response of others, and (3) paramount—inhabited by a sense of utmost significance and value. These three criteria will help us know if we have a worthy Box A—*Ultimate Aim*. Let's take a closer look at each of these features.

···⟩

1. Immediate

Box A—*Ultimate Aims* needs to be attainable in some true measure right now, in the present, at this very moment. We can wait ten years to reach a goal, but we can't wait ten years to have a way of being. We have to show up and be a certain way today. Since essence is revealed in the here and now, the ultimate aim should be pursuable as an *immediate* aim.

What, then, is immediate? How I carry myself is immediate. What I choose to value or emphasize is immediate. My commitment to excellence and the exercise of my voice of advocacy, along with my colleagues, is immediate. The presence I and the others around me bring to our every action and interaction is immediate.

The immediate nature of Box A—*Ultimate Aims* does not keep us from planning for the future; it simply helps us realize that our future depends on a way of being now. We can work for a future response from a client, but we can be faithful to prepare now. We can labor to improve the future habits of healthy living in our communities, but we can be determined to bring the best of ourselves to our work right now. We can employ strategies to engage our employees in the mission, but we can be a model of full engagement now. There is much we look to achieve in others in the future, but all that is predicated on how we are being now.

Having an immediate Box A also means that we can stop ourselves when we realize we are not living or fulfilling our Ultimate Aims and work it out. Our Box A—*Ultimate Aims* is available for instant gutcheck and redress, both individually and organizationally. The *heart* issues of Box A are not necessarily quick or easy to fix; but they can be attended to at any point along the way and attained in some true measure in every moment. Living with fidelity to Box A—*Ultimate Aims* is up to us, which brings us to the second characteristic.

2. Sovereign

A good rule of thumb when developing our Box A — *Ultimate Aims* is to think about whether achieving it depends on the response of others. This is the point where many of us find we need to revise our first-draft statements of Box A. If the aim requires a change in people or circumstance outside of ourselves, it is not yet a Box A. Ultimate aims are best when they are within our power to achieve them, that is to say, within our own sovereignty. This sovereignty aspect allows us to fulfill our Box A—*Ultimate Aims* in any situation and keeps us from excusing or justifying less-than-exemplar attitudes and essence. We have sole agency over our Box A; no one else does. No matter what the circumstance, no matter how the world treats us, we will abide by these aims. Curiously, when liberty and agency appear to have been removed, we often find what we have true sovereignty over.

Václav Havel, the first post-communist president of Czechoslovakia, has unique insight into this element of sovereignty. Before he was thrust into politics in 1989 at the collapse of the Eastern Bloc, he was a professional poet and playwright. Amidst the suffocating rule of the Soviet hegemony during the 1980s he emerged as one of the clearest voices of Eastern European dissidence. Liberty of public discourse had been all but extinguished by the communist party. Havel, writing boldly and brilliantly as a political critic, was first blacklisted and then imprisoned for his public critique. In a letter from prison, he described Box A sovereignty with beautiful clarity:

> When a person chooses to take a certain stand, when he breathes some meaning into his life, it gives him perspective, hope, purpose. When he arrives at a certain truth and decides to "live in it," it is his act and his alone; it is an existential, moral, and ultimately a metaphysical act, growing from the depths of his heart and aimed at filling his own being; from a certain point of view, it is a self-sufficient act, essentially independent

of the shifts and tides in his surroundings…. If such an orientation is true and deep, no change in external conditions and circumstances can alter his choice in its deepest foundations.

Someone who does not draw strength from himself and who is incapable of finding the meaning of his life within himself will depend on his surroundings, will seek the map to his own orientation somewhere outside himself—in some ideology, organization, or society, and then, however active he may appear to be, he is merely waiting, depending. He waits to see what others will do, or what roles they will assign to him, and he depends on them—and if they don't do anything or if they botch things, he succumbs to disillusion, despair, and ultimately, resignation. The sect he belongs to has disappointed him and he collapses like a punctured balloon.

Havel helps us see that we are vulnerable when we make Box A—*Ultimate Aims* dependent on the cooperation of those outside of us—on clients, communities, or colleagues. When our essence—our fundamental sense of who we are and who we will be in all things—begins to depend on others, we compromise a clear and focused mind, a strong and distinctive will, a robust and centered sense of personal or corporate self. We shift and maneuver and weaken as we negotiate and accommodate. This happens to us both individually and organizationally.

Box A offers a way to be true to our ideals no matter how our circumstances unfold, providing both steadiness and agency. It's powerful when a group of frontline staff can say, "In all things, we will bring our best to this work even on the tough days"; when a group of public servants say, "In all things, we will treat people with dignity even when we are not treated with dignity"; or when a group of executives can say, "In all things, we will conduct ourselves honestly and with responsibility toward our employees and our customers even in the toughest circumstances and most cut-throat business climate."

The sovereignty feature of Box A also implies a sequencing of priorities. First, an individual or organization needs to embody its Ultimate Aims before seeking to influence the world. The core nature of an individual or organization—the kind of life it will live, what it will stand for, how its members relate to each other and the world—must be defined before *what* it seeks to accomplish can be secured. Box A—*Ultimate Aims* precedes the vision and mission of Box C—*Intended Impact*. It is perilous to get this order confused.

You've seen it happen in a family system. The love between a parent and child, for instance, is a powerful bond. However, if being loved by a child (a fine Box C—*Intended Impact*) becomes a parent's Box A — *Ultimate Aims*, we have a problem. The child quickly discovers (for no child would miss it!) that he or she has hold of real power—the power to grant or withhold the fulfillment of the *Ultimate Aim*. The parent ends up chasing the child, pulling affirmation from the child, desperately seeking some expression of love from the child. And the child ends up spoiled, demanding, insufferable.

A parent can influence and develop a child's love, but cannot control it. A father and mother can wish and work and strive and strategize to raise a loving child. But truly, at the end of the day, they only can guarantee that they are loving parents. For a parent, "In all things, I will love my child" is a good Box A—*Ultimate Aims*. The parental mission, "I intend to raise a child who will learn to love others, including me," is a wonderful Box C—*Intended Impact*. The distinction is vital in any human system.

Doug McMillan, the CEO of the YMCA of the Triangle, an organization dedicated to making a difference in the communities of the Research Triangle region around Raleigh and Durham, North Carolina, once talked about a Box A—*Ultimate Aim* like this: "In all things, the YMCA will be a pillar in the community." Notice how he didn't say, "We will be recognized as a pillar," or "We will be treated as a pillar," or "We will be the 'go-to' pillar of people's choice." Such an aim would have put his organization in a similar posture to the insecure parent, chasing an elusive public sentiment of popularity or reciprocity or love. Instead, no matter how the community responds, the YMCA can exude steadiness, fortitude, strength, dependability—characteristics of a pillar. They have sovereignty over this aim. It is a sound and solid Box A. His YMCA association has more recently adopted the YMCA brand's voice as their Box A: "In all things we will be genuine, nurturing, welcoming, determined, and hopeful." They have sovereignty over these traits as well.

The sovereign aspect of Box A—the freedom to choose one's highest aim—allowed Havel to promote human dignity even in the face of an oppressive totalitarian regime. It gave Frankl a sense of personhood amidst the horrors of a concentration camp. It allows us to act respectfully toward coworkers and clients who don't treat us with respect. It helps our organizations honor people in the midst of layoffs and cutbacks. It keeps our work groups caring about the prosperity of a whole community and not just our own fiefdoms in the face of mounting competition for limited funds. It helps us individually and collectively find the strength and dignity to be who we need to be even in the face of adversity.

3. Paramount

Box A—*Ultimate Aims* is designed to hold our highest priority, but too often this part of the iceberg erodes from commitments of lesser worth. Each one of us lives for something, whether or not we know it, admit it, examine it, or are intentional about it. Every organization we serve, no matter what its public statements, exists for some ultimate purpose. As we established earlier, the question is not, "Do we have a Box A—*Ultimate Aims*?," but rather, "What is currently filling us, motivating us, balancing us, and against what will we ultimately judge ourselves?" If commitments of lesser value and virtue eat away at our Box A— *Ultimate Aims*, we will find our icebergs tilting precariously in directions we don't intend.

Box A refuses to be unfilled. If not filled intentionally, it will inexorably draw whatever is closest or most frequently talked about into its Box A – place. This phenomenon explains why we sometimes see staff members living ultimately not to make a mistake, or never to look foolish, or always to appear over-worked. They are living for something, just nothing like a sufficient Box A. It is why we find organizations existing ultimately to grow bigger, or to balance the budget, or to have a better reputation in the community than another institution. It is why we discover managers ultimately committed to keeping the peace, or to placating authority, or to never taking risks even when they are in the best interest of the organization. There is nothing wrong with these aspirations per se, they are all simply insufficient as *ultimate* sources of motivation. They are best as secondary, not primary, commitments.

The directors of Johnson & Johnson differentiated between primary and secondary commitments in that meeting two years prior to the Tylenol crisis. When they emerged from the boardroom, they had penned a guiding manifesto holding them to their first responsibility. That is why, when a wave of tragedy crashed into their storied institution, Burke could stand firm and instruct his crisis team to handle questions in the order he did: "How do we first protect the people we serve, and *then* how do we save the product?" And that is why their ultimate aims were experienced throughout the reach of their public influence as a sweet aroma of trustworthiness.

Arranging the order of commitments and determining what is paramount may seem like a minor task, but it proved a determination of no small consequence during September 1982, when fear gripped the minds of thousands who had swallowed a pill, and when a company's future tilted dangerously toward the depths. Establishing primary commitments is no small act for any of us in our personal lives or in our corporate experience. At the end of the day, what matters most for us makes all the difference in how others experience us and how they are moved by us.

Testing Box A

Let's check the Box A of Johnson & Johnson against the three criteria we have established and see how it measures up. *In all things, we will act responsibly first and foremost to doctors, nurses, patients, mothers, and fathers.*

⟩ *Is it immediately accessible?* Yes. At any point and at all times, anyone in the company can stop and ask if their priorities are oriented toward responsibility for the welfare of their customers.

⟩ *Does the company have sovereignty over it?* Yes. This position can be held regardless of the responses of others, regardless of what opinion their clients, stakeholders, or members of the media hold, and regardless of whether others act responsibly.

⟩ *Is it a position of paramount significance?* Yes. The core commitment of any organization is a part of its Box A, and this particular aspiration for Box A is virtuous enough to inhabit an ultimate ideological space.

There is likely more to Johnson & Johnson's ultimate aims. But a commitment like this fits Box A well. As Havel points out, a Box A loyalty is "...an existential, moral, and ultimately a metaphysical act, growing from the depths of [the] heart and aimed at filling [the] being." For Johnson & Johnson, their ultimate aim is a commitment to a particular kind of responsibility. For Doug McMillan at the YMCA of the Triangle, his ultimate aim is a commitment to a way of engaging and being present in the community. For our organizations and initiatives, our ultimate aim may be a commitment to a particular set of values that we collectively determine we will embody no matter what befalls us. For our individual lives, a Box A—*Ultimate Aims* may also be a commitment to a particular kind of priority—not a priority of doing but a priority of being, so that at the end of the day, no matter how the story of our lives unfolds, we may live well.

Practicing Box A

Defining and clarifying Box A—*Ultimate Aims* is only a part of what it takes to move icebergs, however. We have to practice our ultimate aim day in and day out, not simply state it. We need to find a way to become animated by our Box A in everything we do. We also need to intervene in the presence and practice of the Box A among those we seek to serve. Obviously, it takes much more than framing and posting our Box A to a wall, and more than simply presenting the idea of Box A to staff, clients, or constituency. A second-hand Box A is shifty, coming and going capriciously and showing up only when convenient. A disembodied Box A is inert, often seemingly inspiring on paper but elusive and merely aspiration in actuality. As I'm sure you've noticed, the official Box A can be at odds with the true Box A experienced by everyone in the organization and everyone the organization touches. It is tempting to promulgate a virtuous Box A and yet miss the work it takes to make it true and real among us. Having the right ideas on paper is not enough. We need to give ongoing attention and engagement to animate an ultimate aim properly and give it iceberg-moving leverage.

The idea of practicing a mental or psychological posture comes to us from many disciplines—psychology, athletics, religion, health, and wellness. The notion of practice is that when we discipline ourselves time and again to a form, it begins to shape our habits and, in time, our hearts. We change ourselves by regularly fitting ourselves to the practice of an ideal mold. A golfer learns a new swing by breaking down the elements of the swing and molding his or her body to each aspect. A musician learns a new score by breaking down the progression of notes and playing them carefully and in order. Certainly any external form can be void of internal meaning—that's a central idea in this discussion. We don't want to perpetuate meaningless practice. But it's difficult to nurture or renovate internal parts of us over the course of time without some external expression to remind us, help discipline us, correct us, and hold us to our internal commitments.

It had been a long day, part of a long trip, and I am waiting for a plane at the international airport in Los Angeles. I haven't been able to find enough time to use of the hotel health and fitness centers along the way and it has been days since I've had a good workout. I decide to try and apply myself to remedying my inaction during these few moments before boarding my flight. I slip behind the agent's counter and find an inconspicuous place to do some low-impact exercises.

There, behind the counter, I discover a woman of faith. She is on her knees, her forehead touching the carpet, her slight frame bending over in prayer before the red-orange sun dipping low over the tarmac in the distance. And there, discreetly behind the check-in screen, she and I both practice our disciplines. She prays. I do my planks. (Her practice, in my mind, is certainly the more virtuous!) Both of us behave with the recognition that the commitments we value must find a disciplined, ongoing expression in our daily living or we will go un-formed.

Box A—*Ultimate Aims* needs to find ongoing expression if it is to become a driving force and truly characterize our lives and work. A management team at the Providence Medical Group in Portland, Oregon, for instance, begins their meetings by taking turns presenting a reading, usually some kind of Box A—*Ultimate Aims* thought. The reading is often accompanied by commentary, or a few moments of discussion. Sometimes it is simply followed by a pause for quiet reflection. The practice takes only a few moments, but it reminds the hospitals' management team of the source of motives and center of being that should fill and animate them. The practice makes Box A—*Ultimate Aims* everyone's responsibility.

This is but one example of a form to nourish a collective practice of Box A—*Ultimate Aims*. Each of us will have to find what will work best in our context and for our people. It might take a little experimenting to get it right.

Now, let's turn our attention to Box B—*Premises*.

Hints for Developing Box A
Ultimate Aims

1. Finish the sentence, "In all things we...." This exercise keeps the focus on what happens or needs to happen regardless of contingencies or the responses of others.

2. Find a way to nourish Box A. It is a living thing, needing to be fed and watered to keep it alive. Most individuals or organizations with a vibrant Box A have some discipline for ongoing attention to their Box A.

3. Watch for the unstated by true ultimate aims. Remember that what we claim and what is reality is often at odds. Pay particular attention to the intangibles of we and our organizations are being experienced by others. Listen for emphases in conversations. Look for what begins to waft where there is pressure or stress. These will be indicators of the active Box A, no matter what happens to be the spoken Box A.

4. Remember that every human system has a Box A. The key is to discover what is currently functioning as Box A, and then to develop and refine it to become an intentional way of being.

5. Watch out for the temptation to elevate vision and mission to a Box A - *Ultimate Aims* space. If this inclination becomes difficult to suppress, work on developing Box C - *Intended Impact* first, and then step back and envision Boxes A and B.

6. Use the three criteria (immediate, sovereign, and paramount) to clarify and vet the possibilities for a statement of Box A.

4. PREMISES: BOX B

H ow often have you been puzzled by the slow pace of change in the people you lead? If you find yourself at the edge of frustration time and again, you are not alone. Many able and dedicated leaders struggle to effect significant change in their human systems.

> A judge in the family and juvenile court system strives to change the way the system handles children; she urges her colleagues to adapt to the unique needs of each family only to watch them return to formulaic interventions.

> A professor chairing a department at a university attempts to revitalize the quality of teaching among his department's faculty, but he can only manage a few superficial classroom concessions from his professors.

> A senior manager at a national nonprofit tries to help people rethink leadership development; she runs headlong into their tenacious attachment to perpetuate tired manuals and inert training modules.

Do these sound familiar? The specifics of your circumstances might be different, but most likely you face similar challenges.

Let's assume for a moment that you have a solid Box A—*Ultimate Aims*. You're embodying your Ultimate Aims "in all things" and regardless of the response of others. Your essence and that of your team appears to be vibrant. But you've been pulling on your iceberg, and your iceberg is not moving. No urging, maneuvering, pushing, or cajoling seems to be making a difference, at least not the difference you envision. What's going on?

Intractability in human systems is often caused by the ideas of Box B—*Premises*. Down in the murky depths of any human iceberg is a set of premises that hold people in place, sometimes even against their better aspirations. We who are leading the iceberg-moving efforts need to dive into two aspects of premises: (1) diagnose the current beliefs about *context* and (2) engage the underlying *core convictions*. Until we deal with these, we will struggle to help people move or make their progress permanent. We will face a countervailing force from rival premises that threaten to pull the iceberg back to where we started.

Premises are powerful. They are easy to have, but enormously challenging to develop properly and rehabilitate once they are malformed. The challenge with beliefs about context is that we sometimes see least clearly that with which we are most familiar. In other words, we can become so embedded in our context we can no longer discern the most significant patterns of human trajectory around us. The challenge to core convictions is, as Robert Kegan of Harvard suggests, we often don't hold our beliefs; our beliefs hold us. Most of us unintentionally adopt assumptions along the way that, for better or worse, develop into convictions over time and determine how we see and do everything.

Imagine the courage it takes to develop a well-formed Box B—*Premises,* and the power for change it will unleash when we get it right. Imagine also the privilege and significance of intervening in the Box B—*Premises* of others. This is an extremely significant element in the iceberg of any human system.

If Box A—*Ultimate Aims* is about the heart, Box B — *Premises* is about the mind. Box A is shaped by Box B. Box B is animated by Box A. An ultimate aim is a commitment, an aspiration, a vow. A premise is a guiding belief, an affirmation of what is true and real and right. To move human icebergs we will need to dive into both.

Engaging Box B — *Premises* means that we will interact with the assumptions people have about their context as well as the core convictions to which they are either consciously or unconsciously dedicated. Let's explore how to dive into Box B and develop it in people.

PREMISES OF CONTEXT

The year 1991 brought massive upheaval to Central Europe. *Glasnost* (openness) and *Perestroika* (economic reforms) had taken hold in the Soviet Union and throughout its satellite states, punching holes in the political and cultural membrane separating Eastern and Western Europe. The communist edifice known as the Soviet Bloc, indomitable for so long, was crumbling. In its place grew a host of new and emergent capitalistic opportunities and, along with them, an array of nascent social and religious ventures.

Leaders from the evangelical branch of the Christian church, ubiquitous throughout North America but suppressed for decades in Eastern Europe under communism, were quick to respond. For years under the shadow of the iron curtain, evangelical Christians had launched clandestine operations befitting the dark plots of spy novels—smuggling theological literature in hidden compartments under the floorboards of cars, convening secretive events for ministry training deep in remote forests, instigating covert church meetings late at night in dark basements. Their brand of Christianity was illegal under communism; the churches they supported had gone underground and off the grid. But all this changed with the fall of the Soviet Union. For the first time in a generation, they were free to openly support the growth of the newly liberated evangelical Christian church. As they did, an early and logical priority emerged: train leaders for the church. But how do you train leaders? The answer seemed clear. Build religious colleges and seminaries.

A surge of well-heeled Christian educators from the West poured into the regions of the former Soviet Union to establish schools of theology. The advisors and consultants knew their craft. Many were veteran educators who held administrative posts at prestigious universities in the West. They brought an impressive array of credentials and a massive experience-base. Moved by a mission to establish viable training programs for church leadership, they directed the flow of Western money and personnel pouring into Eastern Europe.

With the release of such irrepressible excitement and generous resourcing, expectations were understandably high. It surprised no one to see rapid progress. It was as if a floodgate was lifted, and churches and evangelical denominations large and small rushed to establish schools. Within ten years, over 120 new educational institutions had been built and occupied by administrators and teaching faculties. The number was astonishing for a single decade's effort. However, cracks soon began to show throughout the nascent edifice of church education. In the dash to fill the former Soviet Union with schools, the Western experts had made a major miscalculation.

Signs of the blunder began to appear not long after the din of opening celebrations faded. Schools began to fail, and fail in increasing number over time. By the middle of the second post-communism decade, many buildings stood vacant and seminaries were shutting their doors. The strategy to develop church leaders was unraveling. The well-intentioned religious educators must have been shaking their heads in alarm and bewilderment. "We are good at this," you can almost hear them thinking. "We know what we are doing, and have done this many times before quite successfully. Why is it not working this time?"

Replicating a program is relatively easy; it's a technical challenge that can be worked out even on the other side of the world, even in post-communist countries like Belarus or Moldova or Ukraine. But icebergs move only when leverage is applied to people at their growing edge, and knowing where that growing edge is requires insight into more than just superficial observations about human context. Gaining such insight means that we develop an abiding curiosity about what is driving people and why they are as they are. It means that we cast a clear-eyed gaze at the motivations and dispositions of those we're working with—at the energies, inclinations, aspirations, fears, traditions, and perceptions that comprise their present makeup. It means that we look long enough to see below the iceberg's tip.

When we find context, we know how to design fit. Think about how easy it is to misread context, do what we have done successfully in a different place or time, follow a cue from what we project of ourselves onto the human situation, and get nowhere. We've all done it at one point or another—focused more on our own processes than on the people we intend to serve. If the result of a true perception of context is relevance—a sweet appropriateness, a scratch at the very place of itching need—then misreading context and failing to see the nuance of true need within people often makes us perpetuate what is ill-fitted for them.

I sometimes imagine myself back in high school, and my English teacher, the most widely feared man in the institution, is making a big deal about the difference between assuming and speculating. He commands the classroom from his corner desk. I watch him lift his enormous, silver-haired head that is resting, like it often does, in his swollen hands. "Class, "he growls at us, "tell me the difference between the word, 'assume' and the word, 'speculate'."

It's not uncommon for him to hold such a severe bearing. I heard once that he suffers from an illness that causes his body enormous pain but leaves his mind frightfully sharp, or maybe that is just our way of making sense of what seems to be madness. We can't tell if the question is a malevolent trap, a linguistic bait to ensnare us, or if this lexical distinction is something none of us should miss. In any case, he is obviously worked up about it, and we have no real choice but to go along.

Assuming, he makes the point by jabbing his finger in the air, is reactive, an impulse disconnected from investigation or analysis. Assuming is knee-jerk, a judgment from the place of inattention. It is often more fantasy—what we wish to be the case—than reality. Sometimes it is more autobiographical—what we believe because of how we are doing or feeling at the moment—than verifiable. Assuming, when braced by rival evidence, refuses to reconsider its fixed frame. The mind's already been made up.

Speculating, he adjures, requires that we lean in and explore and question, discover and rediscover. It demands that we shake ourselves from the stupor of our own personal and idiosyncratic narratives and pay attention to others. It forces us to diagnose what is driving people and to concentrate not on our own stories, but on the surrounding world and the undercurrents moving the worlds surrounding others.

I suspect now, years later, that my teacher had been observing teenagers long enough to know our tendency to see others as reflections of ourselves and other people's situations as reflections of our own. I imagine he wanted us to realize that the assumptions we make about context are constructed by our own perspectives and that we tend to assume too much about the world around us. Recently, the lesson is finally beginning to sink in. I find myself wondering: What do we simply assume about our situations and the people in them? What do we miss seeing because we think we already know why people are as they are? How much do we assume simply because we have become accustomed to it?

Familiarity, it seems, can be confused with intimacy, both in our work and our relationships. Instead of sharpening our perception, familiarity sometimes veils our eyes from seeing. We think we truly know below the surface in humans because we are used to seeing above the surface. Could it be that those religious educators from the

West, so familiar with their craft and context, assumed too much? Did they miss the opportunity to take a more sufficient dive into the context of the former Soviet Union precisely because they were educational experts and had become so accustomed to their teaching profession?

I am often surprised by how even modest below-the-surface conversations with people can illuminate surprising features I never imagined or anticipated—even with people and situations I think I know well. Familiarity can make me prematurely dismissive. It can fool me into thinking I understand when I'm actually quite out of touch. In tough circumstances, familiarity can also so make me think, "Change will never happen here, not with these people. This iceberg is going nowhere."

We've heard it said that familiarity breeds contempt, which explains the annoyance we feel when we are over-exposed to the superficial parts of people. It also tends to breed shallow and misleading assumptions. But intimacy—the by-product of deep and abiding curiosity—always enlightens. A deep and abiding curiosity provides an antidote to the numbing assumptions of familiarity. It keeps us engaged. It also usually engenders appreciation even when, on occasion, it is an appreciation of something dark and difficult in which we may need to intervene.

When we apply an ongoing, respectful, and *speculative* curiosity, we are less likely to confuse familiarity with intimacy. We are less apt to adopt strategies that may be perfect for some other context but not for this one, or for a group of people somewhere else or in some other time but not in *this* space or time. We are less tempted to launch an impressive array of programs and products, executed flawlessly of even with a splash of panache, having no power to move our icebergs. We are less prone to miss the *pop*—that burst of excitement when our effort ignites a tinderbox of need, energy, and readiness.

Sometimes we want to adopt a program simply because it sounds good. We hear about an idea, perhaps at a conference or in a book. It produced amazing results for another organization, and we assume it will have the same effect for ours. Eagerly, we put the idea into motion. But no matter how hard we try, no matter how meticulously we follow methods and apply operational metrics, the idea never quite takes hold. We think our problem is execution, and so we train better and tighten our delivery. But in many cases, the problem is not in the idea; instead, it is in the idea's fit. That's what happened in the Christian education initiative across Eastern Europe in the 1990s.

The early surge of Western resources, in most cases, created for the churches in the former Soviet Union an abundance of Western-fitting institutions. The well-meaning educators founded diminutive replicas of successful Western academies, proliferating an idea that had worked for so long on the other side of the globe—the side they were used to seeing, the side with which they were most familiar. We can certainly understand the pressure to take a proven route. You want to meet the magnitude of opportunity with a worthy and winning response. You translate accredited curricula, recruit credentialed professors, place pedigreed administrators, build the traditional brick-and-mortar schools you know how to build. You do what you know works, or at least what you assume will be best.

The strategy played well to Western financiers eager to establish ministerial education for leaders who had previously received only an occasional pamphlet from the trunk of a car or secretly gathered in a forest dacha. It was a safe bet to use tried-and-true best practices. Or so they thought. It all began well, but the surge of momentum lasted for only a few years. Slowly at first, but with gathering frequency throughout the next decade, schools began to empty. The initial flush of interest mysteriously began to drain away. It was a vexing development. You can imagine the scratching of heads: "What is wrong? How are we not executing?" The problem, however, was not one of execution.

In 2005, a group led by a visionary and gregarious Russian expatriate, Sergey Rakhuba, gave it a fresh look. Rakhuba had immigrated to the United States for religious freedom during the darkest days of communist hegemony and settled in suburban Chicago. For years he had been shuttling back and forth to the regions of the Former Soviet Union, even before the fall of the iron curtain, to aid in the revitalization of the evangelical Christian church. He and others recognized that the future of their church depended on preparing a new generation of leaders.

They quickly saw that Western premises of context were wrong. The post-communist climate of the Former Soviet Union differed radically from Western socioeconomic and cultural realities. In the former Soviet regions, students couldn't afford to pay hefty sums for tuition like their Western counterparts. They were disinclined to leave their homes to study in a distant city. An isolated and protracted course of academia, so familiar in the West, was simply untenable for most young people. To complicate matters further, job options in the church were severely limited for new graduates. The assumptions undergirding a Western, formal approach to education simply didn't fit.

Rakhuba and his group broke through the prevailing assumptions to gain renewed insight into context and design a fresh and fitting response. They developed the notion that an educational model should be grounded in churches instead of schools, oriented around cadres of students who were embedded in local parishes, resourced by scholar-practitioners with local ties, organized in smaller units scattered more liberally around the region, and focused on social action and community service. Free from the tether of Western assumptions, they designed a new and bold iceberg-moving approach. Their School Without Walls, as it came to be called, *popped*. Within four years, they had established 41 sites with an astonishing participation of more than 3,000 students annually, far exceeding the reach of their formal educational counterparts. They now can hardly keep up with the surge of interest, excitement, and energy.

It is during the long, heavy days of a Ukrainian summer, and I am perched on the bench seat of a travel van, mashed next to Rakhuba, four of his Russian associates, and a film crew from the United States documenting the progress of School Without Walls. I am along at the behest of a Chicago-based foundation to evaluate the educational design of the model. For two weeks we are touring School Without Walls sites, navigating the vast expanses between remote Ukrainian towns, bumping over broken roads creased with bone-shaking crevasses. The face of culture is quick to adjust to a new era, but infrastructure in some of these regions still bears a sad legacy of long-term communist neglect.

What strikes me most, as we travel from meeting to meeting packed with earnest, socially active, religiously developing young people, is a sense of the model's fit and congruence with context. There is nothing particularly noteworthy about the content of the project, or its administration, or even its execution. From a design standpoint the primary feature of brilliance is obvious: the model fits the human context perfectly. Fit tends to elevate even a modest program to exceptionality.

Fitting our efforts to context is no small matter, but we eventually need more than fit if we intend to make a difference. If context is all we have in Box B, we will be tied to what is the present reality. We will be forced along by the tide and trends of the moment. We will commit what philosophers call the naturalistic fallacy: defining what ought to be by what is the case. The context dimension of Box B needs a counterweight, a more stable and secure feature to act as ballast, something to hold it steady. Box B needs deep conviction to keep it from turning into a frenetic chase for an ephemeral fit. Box B needs core convictions.

Hints for Developing
Premises of Context

1. Use qualitative methods to gain deeper perspective. It's easy to use an average from a survey as a basis for context, but this is often a thin and undifferentiated measure. There is still so much we do not know about how our employees are doing even after we get 3.2 out of 5 on a staff-satisfaction survey, for instance. Qualitative data, gathered from guided conversations, disciplined observations, and the artifacts of the human residue left in other humans from interactions will give us deeper insight.

2. Beware of appealing to anecdotes as if they were evidence. We see something, or hear about something, and draw broad conclusions from the singular story. Remember, the plural of anecdote is not data. Even a few anecdotes are highly unreliable sources from which to draw conclusions about context. We have to inquire more substantially.

3. Perform solid data analysis before drawing conclusions. Good data, both quantitative and qualitative, is immensely useful, but only if interpreted well.

4. Develop a regular discipline of inquiry to keep a finger on the changing pulse of context. Developing collective habits of reflection can be highly educative for all involved.

5. Remember that everyone is constructing perceptions about context that are taken for reality. It is helpful to engage these assumptions when renovating the Box B – *Premises of Context* in people.

Premises of Core Convictions

The second dimension of Box B, *core convictions*, holds weight and influence similar to Box A. Beliefs matter. They may be unseen, but to a great extent they determine our *telos*, where our trajectory ultimately will land us. Beliefs cause us to do what we do, or avoid what we avoid, both organizationally and personally. They are potent but often (and quite surprisingly) unspoken and unexamined. If we can corner these beliefs, if we can test how true they are in practice, we will have a better chance at redesigning them and making a lasting difference in ourselves and others. Like context, core convictions lie low in the iceberg. Core convictions influence how we see context; context challenges and sharpens our core convictions.

The primary task of this part of Box B is to answer the question: *To what beliefs are we dedicated?* Notice it is not, To what methods or strategies are we committed? Nor is it, To what mission are we committed? Instead, the core convictions feature of Box B – *Premises* requires us to access and clarify the ideas that sit below our mission and strategy. The question may take other forms: What do we believe about the nature of people? What do we believe that makes us able to bear our mission well? What do we believe to be beautiful and good and valuable? What do we believe to be most threatening? In a way, the second dimension of Box B is still about context. From this angle, however, it is the context of the beliefs that encase us. We hold these beliefs, but more significantly, these beliefs hold us.

Whether spoken or unspoken, deliberate or unintentional, beliefs determine how things will be and what will become of us. For example, a senior manager at a large and respected nonprofit recently exclaimed in a staff meeting how much the belief that "people are basically dishonest" had crept into their membership policies, giving an adversarial tone to the experience of member engagement. A former executive at a tech company is known for constantly voicing the belief that "only the paranoid survive" in the vicious climate of high-technology design, giving a frenetic energy to the company's ethos. The founders of the Container Store believe that "all employees are partners," giving a sense of shared ownership to everyone from entry-level personnel all the way to the executive suite. Beliefs determine the movement or stasis of icebergs, for better or worse. Beliefs have consequences.

Box B beliefs can be rich, deep, and moving. Take, for instance, the tagline for the Bill and Melinda Gates Foundation: *Dedicated to the idea that all people deserve the chance to live healthy, productive lives.* The Gates Foundation is rooted in two additional beliefs that inform all philanthropic work:

··❯ *All lives—no matter where they are being lived—have equal value.*

··❯ *To whom much is given, much is expected.*

Here are some stated core beliefs of other organizations:

··❯ *It is in our nature to innovate.* (Nike, Inc.)

··❯ *Understanding world geography as a youth is a prerequisite to acting with global responsibility as an adult.* (The National Geographic Association)

··❯ *Every child has value and deserves the opportunity to grow in spirit, mind, and body.* (Calgary YMCA Youth Workers)

··❯ *All people are worthy.* (City of Surrey, Department of Community and Recreational Services)

These statements, if truly held, will permeate people and shape the work. They will steady people as well, keeping them from tipping over in the tempest, like a deep keel on a tall sailing ship, or the weighty mass of an iceberg that sits under the water.

The core convictions of Box B also protect us from seeking relevance to such excess that we forget who we are and what we stand for. It stops the creeping debilitation caused by chasing the idea *du jour.* Eagerness to pursue a trend can unwittingly make us to unravel wholeness and congruence within our work. Even with the best logic models, tightly defined outcomes and impact measures, and carefully honed tactics, we can drift off course without core convictions. Organizational culture can get co-opted by whatever is new and exciting, or whatever personality is loudest and most persuasive, or whatever happens to be the most urgently felt pressure of the moment. We can lose our sense of who we want to be.

Organizational culture is defined as much by core convictions as anything else. A strong and healthy culture requires a strong and healthy set of core beliefs that pervade and animate all of us in all we do. Without core beliefs, we struggle to stay together and be productive. Without them, we have to navigate unspoken and often inconsistent beliefs, tossed by the swirling forces of conflicting institutional agendas. We have to spend a lot of time and energy trying to decipher what's really important and to whom. Without a common Box B, we can sit in the same staff meeting and hear the same speech and yet walk away with our heads in entirely different places. Without congruence in Box B, communication can become spectacularly confusing. However, with a robust and embedded set of shared beliefs, we have the chance to form a clear and stable culture from which we may inhabit our mission convincingly.

Along with providing a true source of culture, core convictions can renovate strategic presence. If the beliefs that are can be named, then the conversation about beliefs which *ought to be* can begin. Because beliefs moor the work, tethering it in place, a change of beliefs frees us to move and advance and develop a strategic edge. New beliefs can provide new leverage to move the iceberg forward. This is how many organizations redevelop and revitalize themselves. Take, for instance, the dramatic reformation of the Missouri Juvenile Programs for Correction.

Late in the 1990s Missouri's juvenile justice system was suffering. Despite all efforts, kids in corrections were languishing. The challenge was not unique to Missouri at the time. Correctional facilities across the country were bulging at the seams, and youth everywhere were becoming increasingly impassive and incorrigible. From the perspective of case workers, the situation was growing dire. During the 1980s, the frequency of arrests for juvenile violent crime had accelerated alarmingly across the United States, and no one quite understood the reasons for the surge. The graphs that tracked youth crime looked like the front edge of a steep grade up a mountain road, rising sharply and heading into the stratosphere.

After a peak in the volume of serious juvenile incidents during 1994, however, the trajectory of violent crimes tipped and began to drop dramatically. Surprisingly however, even as the number of violent crimes began to plummet, rates of juvenile incarceration continued to soar. The statistics were incongruous: increasingly more kids were being locked up for increasingly lesser crimes. Between 1994 and 2003, even as juvenile arrests for violent crime offenses (murder, rape, robbery, and aggravated assault) fell 48 percent to its lowest level since 1980, the incarceration rates (the number of kids taken into custody) continued to sky-rocket. The *War on Drugs* in the late 1980s and the *Gun-Free Schools Act of 1994* were emblematic of a hardening public sentiment toward young offenders and fueled zero-tolerance policies within schools. Kids with disciplinary problems formerly handled at school were now being handed over to the police. The message was clear: it's time to get tough. But what, then, do you do with all those kids you have taken into custody?

Missouri's correctional system, like most across the country, scrambled to put together a plan to handle the burgeoning population of incarcerated youth. They decided to build a capacious rural facility able to house 2,500 young people. It was modeled after the traditional penal settings for adults that you see on occasion when you drive through remote, out-of-the-way places. Their strategy was to remove young offenders from the city, place them in a single, isolated location and employ on them the strictest, most punitive correctional methods. It was a hardline approach designed to demonstrate a serious commitment to turn the tide of juvenile delinquency. Their strategy was efficient, impressive, and, to the view of many observers, largely ineffective. The tougher they got, the more recalcitrant youth became.

Puzzled by the darkening situation, a group of key leaders from the Children's Defense Fund representing various parties throughout the region's juvenile correctional community, sat down to try and help solve the growing problem. They decided to ask themselves a Box B—*Premises of Core Convictions* question, "Who do we believe kids to be, fundamentally, in their nature?" They had a hunch that the beliefs they held, or perhaps more accurately, the beliefs that were holding them, might explain their inability to gain traction on the problem. And they were right. The answer to their Box B question changed everything.

After difficult soul-searching, they identified some surprising and previously unexpressed (or possibly, suppressed) beliefs:

⋯⟩ Children are good.

⋯⟩ Children can learn and grow and change.

⋯⟩ Children can be empowered with a sense of hope.

⋯⟩ Accountability and internalized change are important.

⋯⟩ Safety and relationships are key.

⋯⟩ The recognition that "from the last he is man, but from the front he is a child."

While we may take issues with some of these beliefs—like whether or not we believe that children are wholly good or, perhaps more accurately, that every child has the capacity for good—it is clear that if these beliefs were adopted, they would dramatically impact the direction of youth intervention. We can see how this new-and-improved Box B—*Core Convictions* could drive a massive overhaul in Missouri's approach to juvenile detention. Indeed, it began to transform their ability to positively impact kids.

Change came dramatically. Instead of packing young troublemakers into a rural compound, they established 33 separate residential facilities and 11 day-treatment centers in five regions. These hubs were de-signed to provide a dormitory atmosphere for smaller groups of no more than 12 teens. They decided that no young person would be housed more than two hours from his or her home to retain a sense of connection with family and community. They did away with isola-tion rooms and the term "correction officer," replacing them instead with youth counselors and team leaders in home-like environments appointed with bunk beds, pillows, couches, and carpets. Other trap-pings from the penal system were jettisoned in favor of a more youth-sensitive touch—personal clothing for youth, education and job train-ing programs, and mandatory participation in community service.

Most importantly, the way they related to young people began to change. Beliefs shape how people interact with people, regardless of the physical environment. Barry Krisberg, the president of the Nation-al Council on Crime and Deliquency makes this point: "The basic log-ic…is that if you treat young people like inmates, they'll act like pris-oners. If you treat them like young people capable of being citizens, they'll much more likely act like citizens." The new, boldly articulated beliefs sharply diverted them from conventional, "get tough" methods of incarceration and containment. For the Department of Youth Ser-vices in Missouri, renovated core beliefs caused a shift in philosophy from confinement to treatment and from corrections to rehabilitation. A revision of Box B—*Premises of Core Convictions*—beliefs about "who kids are" refreshed the entire system. The old set of beliefs, perhaps not fully examined, had been holding them back. With new beliefs, the iceberg was free to move.

The numbers show an impressive effect. A renovation of beliefs actually gave them a massive ROI:

⋯⟩ Recidivism dropped to less than 8%, one of the best rates na-tionally.

⋯⟩ Youth incarcerations in one progressive prison were reduced during a five year period by 7 to 8% annually.

···〉 Ninety-one percent of youth earned high school credits in this system compared to 46% in traditional facilities.

Their model is now widely emulated. Today, throughout the juvenile justice community of North America, this approach is commonly called the "Missouri Way."

To fundamentally change ourselves, our organizations, or those we serve, we must closely examine and renovate those ideas we hold to be most fundamental. We sometimes avoid talking about them because we assume these beliefs are personal and private. But convictions always affect our public expressions. Even though we might feel discomfort talking to our colleagues about core beliefs, the process can be powerfully persuasive if done with sensitivity and respect. If we can collectively renovate our core convictions, no matter how slight the renovation, we will succeed in detaching the anchor of the old and delivering possibility of the new. In some cases, changing beliefs will set into motion a cascade of revisions that will dislodge even the most formidable icebergs.

Renovating core convictions takes some diligence, however. Writing beliefs on a brochure or posting them on a website rarely makes people actually *believe* differently. Stating beliefs is the easy part. Getting people to actually believe is another matter. Too often, our stated beliefs are inert. And as Alfred North Whitehead has written, "Inert ideas are ideas that have not been utilized, tested, or thrown into fresh combinations." We will need to examine the assumptions surrounding our beliefs, work out the implications of our beliefs, and test them in a variety of possible applications before they gain power to animate us.

The key to developing a productive set of convictions is to think not only of the most seminal precepts, but also to consider the ones we are in most danger of abandoning when the going gets tough. In Homer's *Odyssey,* King Odysseus, returning from the Trojan War and desperate to be reunited with his family and see his homeland, ties himself to the mast of his ship to guard against the seductive Siren's song and keep himself from diving overboard or running his ship aground in their pursuit. He lashes himself to the ship's mast in an admission that his power of reasoning and clarity of thinking might be overwhelmed at the time of heightened stress. In other word, he couldn't trust himself, in the Siren-filled moment, to keep a clear head.

Our most powerful core convictions are those to which we commit ourselves long before our most trying days, as if we, like Odysseus, were lashing ourselves to an ideological mast. They are the beliefs we preemptively determine to hold, knowing we will be tempted to let go of them during times of discomfort and distraction, threat and seduction. They are the beliefs we determine to hold no matter how circumstances appear. If we only state benign or sentimental beliefs, beliefs that will cost us nothing to hold, we will have missed the opportunity to think strategically about our Box B. Instead, we need to anticipate what we will most likely lose sight of in the heat of our work or jettison when we are pressed. Then, we lash ourselves to those beliefs.

Time and again those at the Bill and Melinda Gates Foundation remind themselves, and everyone listening, that they are "dedicated to the idea that all people deserve the chance to live healthy, productive lives." Why this core belief? And why do they keep stating it publicly? Could it be they anticipate that in the global theater of charity they might be tempted to value some people and some regions of the world more than others, hence the words "all people"? Could they imagine an inclination to focus on the more scintillating arena of human health but not the more mundane arena of human productivity, hence the use of both words "healthy" and "productive"? Central to what it means to be human, they are convinced, is the opportunity not just for a healthy life, but a productive one as well. They have committed the organization and themselves to this idea, and thereby stay the course.

Let's review the ideas of Box B — *Premises.*

Having good premises of context ensures that we will be relevant to our operating environment. We will keep our eye on the people we serve and anticipate how their shifting iceberg might affect the evolution of our interventions. We will have feedback loops to illuminate the cracks in our connectivity to current need. We will know how to touch people at their growing edge.

Having good premises of core convictions secures both a timeless, steady sense of depth for us and the power to move others deeply. We will rework our shared and guiding ideas to give us a point of iceberg-moving leverage. We will test the depth of their penetration against our impulses and inclinations. Along the way, we will discover a balance and stability—a ballast to keep us and those around us upright and buoyant.

Let's now turn our attention to determining what kind of difference we want to make, our Box C — *Intended Impact*.

Hints for Developing
Premises of Core Convictions

1. Focus on developing a handful of key beliefs. People won't be able to remember a long litany of beliefs. Take care to emphasize just a few of the most salient and productive beliefs needed to keep properly oriented. Core convictions need to be usable, and for them to be usable they have to be few, memorable, and meaningful.

2. Test the presence of core convictions by looking at the natural impulses and inclinations of the group. The deep assumptions that are fueling tendencies in our actions are often at odds with our stated beliefs. An honest look is often quite revealing.

3. Try not only to state the beliefs that cost you nothing; state the beliefs you will be tempted to ignore and those ideas to which you should be dedicated that you also suspect will be sorely tested. These will be the beliefs to hold onto with all your might. The most productive beliefs are the ones that are risky to state, the ones at the edge of our collective competency.

4. Explore the possibility that you may be holding a core conviction or two that you really don't intend to hold, ones that are causing complications. Most of us, both individually and collectively, have adopted assumptions along the way that get us into trouble and cause us to act or react in unproductive ways.

5. Think through the implications of the beliefs and how you might hold them more fully. Nominating beliefs is easy. Deciding which should be emphasized is a bit more difficult. Actually coming to conviction about your stated beliefs is even more challenging. Think about collective and ongoing rehearsal, working out and practicing their implications, testing them time and again, exploring rival beliefs, examining threats to these beliefs, and generating processes to move the ideas from statements on paper to convictions embedded in the heart.

5. INTENDED IMPACT: BOX C

The year 1961 was one of simmering social unrest across the United States, particularly within race relations throughout the South. For years various activists and organizations had been pushing on the iceberg of racial inequality only to find virulent and implacable pockets of resistance to change. Racial mores had become deeply entrenched in the culture, fortified by generations of attitudes and behaviors at odds with a fundamental premise on which the nation had been founded, a core conviction that *all people are created equal.* Finally, discontent and conscience had ripened in enough people and the time to confront the malformed social constructs of racial injustice was at hand.

On November 9, in Albany, Georgia, a young group of student activists, calling themselves the Student Nonviolent Coordinating Committee (SNCC), met to propose a new chapter in the nascent civil rights movement. Their handbill was drafted by Charles Sherrod, a young Virginian who had turned down a plum college faculty appointment to serve a movement that held promise for more social consequence than could be had by any singular academic career.

Sherrod's handbill illustrates beautifully how Box B—*Core Convictions* can come alive in Box C—*Intended Impact.* He begins with the SNCC's fundamental beliefs and then articulates the implication of these beliefs in the context of the 1960s United States, setting the trajectory of what would become one of the most powerful and esteemed social movements in the country's history:

> We believe in the Fatherhood of God and the brotherhood of man. We believe that God made of one blood all nations to dwell on all the face of the earth. If we are of one blood, children of one common Father, brothers in the household of God, then we must be of equal worth in His family, entitled to equal opportunity in the society of men.... We are called upon, therefore, to love our fellow men, all of them, with all the risks that that implies and all the privileges that it promises.

A few months later, on April 29, 1962, Sherrod and other SNCC personnel met to crystallize their vision and resolved to create "a social order permeated by love and to the spirituality of nonviolence." They committed to establish "a circle of trust, a band of sisters and brothers gathered around the possibilities of agapeic love, the beloved community." These statements, among others, spelled out the effect they wanted the SNCC to have on their neighborhoods. It was a daring vision of change for the South and even more broadly, the whole of society in the 1960s. It was a bold and powerful Box C—*Intended Impact.*

Activists of the Civil Rights movement, keen to see social transformation take hold and reconstitute racial rights, rallied around clear and compelling visions like the SNCC's and similar articulations of purpose from groups like the Congress of Racial Equality (CORE), the Council of Federated Organizations (COFO), and others associated with Martin Luther King, Jr. The seemingly intractable iceberg of racial injustice needed to be moved. The idea that a nation could uphold and protect the rights of all of its citizens, regardless of race and ethnicity, or even gender, age, and a host of other orientations or limitations that draw social discrimination, galvanized and mobilized perhaps the greatest social movement in the history of the nation, resulting in the enactment and enforcement of the Civil Rights Act of 1964.

As with the American Civil Rights Movement, most great endeavors of social change are catalyzed by notions of where they are going and what the future will look like when they get there. This is the power of Box C—*Intended Impact.*

Developing the idea of intended impact

Since a clear notion about impact is essential to moving an iceberg of people, how do we develop a Box C—*Intended Impact* that's compelling enough to draw employees, volunteers, clients, and communities and help them to pour their lives into a cause? How do we, like the leaders of the Civil Rights Movement during the 1960s, frame a vision for impact such that others will rise up to join the iceberg-moving effort? We might imagine that the value of our cause is self-evident, that all we need to do is show up and present it well, but neither personality nor presentation will be enough if we haven't a clear and compelling substance to our call.

Take, for instance, the plight of a local, ethnic-heritage foundation. It recently found itself in a financial corner, struggling to meet payroll. Members of the executive committee were in the midst of planning their annual board retreat and faced the choice of either clarifying the unique impact they were intending to have or designing a fundraising plan to meet the urgent payroll need. Since they had only limited time and energy, they decided to stick with a fundraising focus. Their choice was understandable. The problem however, was that they still had no compelling case for why people should join their cause. They had yet to give a clear call to an intended impact. Boards need fundraising plans, but they first need an idea about the good that will be secured in the community by the organization, a clear sense of what those funds will attain, beyond simply the perpetuation of the institution.

Such calls to impact are tough to form well. Consider two common pitfalls to avoid when drawing people to Box C—*Intended Impact.*

Pitfall #1: Focusing on ideas about "us"

First, we tend to think more about goals for our achievement than to picture our impact on others. We tend to focus on how to gain greater market penetration, increase in size by a certain percentage, establish more programs, and move the needle on our performance instead of envisioning how the community will be different, what clients or constituencies will have gained, and which capacities will be strengthened in those we serve. Naturally, we care about the reputation of our work. We care about the quality of our performance and the scale of our achievements. However, Box C—*Intended Impact* is supposed to be about the difference we intend to make in others. It is fundamentally others-centered. Impact is about them, not us.

A colleague and I found ourselves speaking for the board of a prominent charity that was meeting at a strikingly picturesque mountain retreat in the Rockies. Noted business and community leaders were in attendance, hailing from a wide range of professional sectors. All appeared highly vested in the organization. To start the weekend, the board moderator offered an introductory word. With the help of a slide to keep the idea front and center, she began, "Our primary aim is to be seen as the premier social service agency in our community." My colleague and I exchanged quick glances. How do you gently and respectfully help a well-intentioned board see that such a focus is organizationally narcissistic? As the primary aim, this idea inclines people to seek position and perception around the community instead of difference in the community. It favors competition instead of collaboration among partners. It is fundamentally about the charity and not about their impact. After a little work, the board came around to embrace the powerful notion of how the community should be different as a result of their presence.

The board's mistake is an easy and honest one to make. For a moment, think through your personal or organizational statements of purpose, mission, vision, and cause—not all of them, just the ones you remember off the top of your head—and see how many of these have to do with your own performance instead of the change you are trying to effect in others. Developing metrics about performance and staying accountable to those are essential management practices, but more appropriate for Box E—*Action* than Box C—*Intended Impact*. How we hold ideas matters. Our tendency to fill Box C—*Intended Impact* with *us* instead of *them* is one of the reasons Box C is labeled "*intended impact*" instead of "organizational goals" or "institutional objectives." Statements about us are important, but they should follow our ideas of intended impact in others. This is the first kind of error.

Pitfall #2: Failing to develop our ideas of impact

A second kind of error is the underdevelopment of ideas about impact. Notions of impact need to mature and ripen before they find lasting resonance within people. We tend to rely on imprecise and undifferentiated slogans to guide us, leaving us with warm feelings but little clarity. Slogans sound clever and tidy, but their meanings are often ambiguous. It's quite challenging for a group to agree on *exactly* what we mean when we say things like, "We want to make a difference in people's lives," "We exist to make the world a safer place for the next generation," or "We are building strong foundations for communities." Do those around us know what we *mean* when we say it? Do we know what we mean when we say it? Ambiguity in Box C—*Intended Impact* creates a cavity in the organizational iceberg, destabilizing it by dispersing people's focus and energy. A vague notion of impact leaves us fumbling for the kind of incisive vision that captured and crystallized the intent of the Civil Rights Movement during its early years.

Vagaries propagate partly because we want to find common ground with as many people as possible, and so we let our words get watered down to mean many things, and partly because our own thinking is not incisive about what we intend to see achieved in the lives of those we serve. You may have heard of new employee orientations emphasizing missions like this: "to help people and businesses throughout the world realize their full potential," or "to be the best in the eyes of our customers, employees and shareholders," or to participate in "bringing the best to everyone we touch." These are all real statements from new employee training programs at large and well-known corporations. They hold fine sentiment, and have a Box A— *Ultimate Aims* ring to them. They indicate sincerity and benevolence. But in the desire to say everything they say nothing. While ideas like these need more precision, they also need to be developed far enough to have lasting meaning for people. Until ideas of impact can resound within heads and hearts, people tend to wander in their own mental meadows, not knowing exactly where they should head.

Relying on slogans can be very confusing for those we lead, for when they hear us using words, even familiar words, what comes to their minds may be quite different than what is in our own. Most of us picture different things when we hear the same thing, and even when our pictures agree, we often have different ideas about what those pictures mean. We hold rival understandings of what impact should look, feel, behave, and end up like. Peter Senge of M.I.T. reminds us of the power of mental models to import meaning to our perspectives. Our individual mental models, products of our own experiences and expectations, send us in different directions even when we gather around a shared slogan and espouse a common statement of mission. The work of Box C—*Intended Impact,* therefore, is to develop a collective intentionality among us, and through us in others.

Components of a Compelling Intended Impact

For the Civil Rights Movement, the ideas of Box C — Intended Impact were composed by a virtuoso. On August 28, 1963, Martin Luther King Jr. mounted the steps of the Lincoln memorial and proclaimed an irrepressible vision:

···> I have a dream that one day on the red hills of Georgia the sons of former slaves and the sons of former slave owners will be able to sit down together at the table of brotherhood.

···> I have a dream that one day even the state of Mississippi, a state sweltering with the heat of injustice, sweltering with the heat of oppression, will be transformed into an oasis of freedom and justice.

···> I have a dream that my four little children will one day live in a nation where they will not be judged by the color of their skin but by the content of their character.

In the cauldron of social unrest in the seething South during the 1960s, people needed a tangible idea of what the future could look like. They needed to become gripped by an articulation of Box C—*Intended Impact*. Dr. King's words were poetry, vivid and visceral. They have become some of the most oft-quoted phrases and enduring imagery from among this nation's public speeches. They drew people of all kinds to the iceberg-movement of social justice.

Many of us dream of causing similar outpouring of human achievement and social effect in our own spheres of influence. Too often, however, we mount our steps, give our speech. We think it's clear and compelling, a call that none should ignore. And then, to our chagrin, some whom we lead just go through the motions, displaying less passion and more languor than we expect. Others seem filled with personal agendas, visions and missions of their own making, individual and proprietary Box C—*Intended Impacts* that have little to do with our collective intent. Still others appear perpetually distracted by minor and temporal tangents of lesser importance, unable to distinguish true impact from the veneer of their own daily activity. Our call to impact needs further development to galvanize the energy of our people.

To engage people with Box C—*Intended Impact,* we have to think together deeply enough about the essence of impact and thoroughly enough to grow the ideas into maturity. We need to explicate three levels of ideas:

···> **Essential Impact.** What is the core and essence of the change we desire to cause? What are the ideas' sine qua non? What are the direct, instead of indirect, targets of our effect? What are the essential changes in others we cannot do without? How does our mission and vision inform our core intention of human impact?

···> **Outcomes.** What are the key elements of our core ideas of impact? What are the critical features of our essential impact? What else might masquerade as impact and seduce us into thinking we have secured impact when, in fact, we have left nothing significant or lasting?

···> **Indicators.** What are the measurable metrics as well as the immeasurable but essential tell-tale signs? What might be stages of impact, levels of change that might not be ultimately satisfying but might still be reliable indicators of true development? What are the signs and signals that we pay attention to in order to determine if we are making progress toward our outcomes?

Once we have developed these notions, we will need to design ways to engage people with this intended impact. We will then begin to see the effects of a collective sense of cause on the icebergs of human systems around us. Let's take a closer look at each level.

Essential Impact

The primary work of Box C—*Intended Impact* is to develop the essential ideas of impact and then embed them within people. These ideas capture our high-level purpose, center our attention on what truly matters, and concentrate our collective energy. They keep everyone's effort focused on a common target and keep aimless distraction and wasteful adventurism locked out. They specify the particular na-ture of our intended contribution and keep us from embracing "any good cause" or other endeavors contrary to our primary pursuit, even if there is once-in-a-lifetime opportunity in front of us or money from funders on the table. They keep our efforts potent, undiluted, and true. High-level Box C—*Intended Impact* posits the *raison d'être* – our reason for being: why we bring this particular group of people to this particular place at this particular time to accomplish *this* end above all others. It is our billboard message, the marquee of our intent.

This job of keeping our eyes on the essential ideas of our intended impact may seem so simple, but it takes vigilance to embed a clear notion of what we are trying to achieve in the hearts and minds of our-selves and others. Box C—Intended Impact is not fully formed until it is rooted in the people who are being gathered to move the iceberg. A written document, no matter how well-written, is often insufficient. It's why many mission statements are benign and forgettable—people can't connect with the statement. Without the ideas coming alive with-in people, intended impact gets lost in an encroaching Box E—Action, and the pursuit of performance eclipses the notion of what impact that performance is intended to achieve.

1. Form engaging ideas.

To construct ideas that will have the greatest chance of engaging people, it's helpful to make them sticky, resonant, and generative:

···> **Sticky.** Ideas need to stick with people if they are ever going to take hold in them. Make the ideas memorable, not simply comprehensive or technically correct. People have to hold key ideas in their minds if they are to be guided by them in the midst of a cause-driven flurry. To accomplish this, try using the evocative imagery of a metaphor, or the audible ring of well-turned phrases, or a communiqué elegant in its simplic-ity, or the surprise of an unexpected pairing of ideas. Start

with ideas stated correctly, if blandly, then play with them creatively, comparing the end product with the original to ensure
no creep. However it is done, stickiness is essential if ideas are
to hang around long enough to guide people.

···> **Resonant.** When we ask, "Does this resonate with you?," we
are usually asking if the ideas are meaningful, if there is a
personal connection and draw. Ideas of impact should move
us. They should be readily identifiable and motivating to us,
even if they are outside our immediate context. If developed
well, like-minded people will be able to identify personally
and quickly with an intended impact. Remember, ideas of impact that either meet a unique need or meet a need uniquely
tend to resonate best with people.

···> **Generative.** The best ideas of impact will have the capacity
to generate further thinking. They will draw from a deep well
of meaning and evoke a rich and robust understanding. They
will be educative and catalytic. They will push people to think
more clearly and substantively about the cause. When formed
well, we will be able to unpack each of them and use them as
a basis for instructing others about what we are all about.

The Province of Alberta contains the vibrant industry of Canadian
oil and gas production. Calgary, its largest city, is home to the major-
ity of management and deal-making. Since growth in the oil and gas
sector has been on a tear over the past decade, the neighborhoods of
greater Calgary have been burgeoning. The Calgary YMCA is stretching to serve a rapidly expanding and increasingly diverse population.
Two new facilities are coming online in the next year—a multi-pur-
pose YMCA in a multi-ethnic neighborhood, a partnership with the
public library, the city, and the North East Centre of Community; and
a YMCA embedded in a new health complex designed to serve patients and health care workers. It's an important time to be clear about
what kind of impact they intend to achieve.

In light of their expanding presence in the community, the YMCA leadership team decided to re-engineer high level Box C—*Intended Impact*. They set aside some time to contemplate exactly what mark they intended to leave on their communities. The more they wrestled with the essence of their intended accomplishments, the more a few simple, yet powerful ideas surfaced. In their minds, it boiled down to four elegant ideas of impact: that the Calgarians they serve would come to **belong**—*make lifelong connections,* **grow**—*continually choose to develop,* **thrive**—*discover what inspires you and take action,* and **lead**—*help others to create positive change.* These are their guiding ideas of impact with sticky phrases to communicate the kernel of each idea in a memorable way. These notions of impact are sticky because they are comprised of only four simple but powerful ideas, resonant because people immediately connect with the need for this kind of development in their communities, and generative because each key word is embedded with an endless potential to be educative.

Consequently, everything they do—every program, every staff training event, every community collaboration, every new health facility, every child program or youth camp—is designed to cause people to grow, thrive, lead, and belong. Even the bus ride that takes children to camp, which used to be a simple experience of transportation, has been re-engineered by the notion of how to use the time in service to children growing, thriving, leading, and belonging. Whether a program is designed for children or adults, singles or families, immigrants or First Nations, if it is not in service to those ends, it is revised or cut. The idea of intended impact holds the potential to engender a collective focus of attention.

2. Engage people with engaging ideas

The Vice President of Children and Youth Strategy at the Calgary YMCA is a bright and energetic YMCA veteran named Tanis Cochrane. She initially trained to be a school teacher, but found herself drawn to the energy and ethos of non-formal education and community service. She was only a year or two out of university when she left the teaching profession to begin working with children through the Calgary YMCA. Now she leads a team that reaches out to children and youth throughout the sprawling metropolis.

Cochrane invited me to join her management team and develop a strategy for engaging their staff, members, partners, and sponsors with ideas of impact. Figuring out a way to engage stakeholders broadly in the vision for impact seemed like a wise and timely move to me. The best ideas, even when stated well, will be inert unless people begin to interact with them authentically. So how do you help people truly engage ideas and not just receive them as they are told?

It is a crisp autumn afternoon and the radiant sun is leaning low in the Canadian sky. We gather around a folding table in a temporary office of one of the expanding facilities. The light angles sharply by the wall of windows as we lean in to devise a plan to illuminate ideas of impact in the minds of people. It ends up looking like this:

1. Identify a group of key leaders from across the association to act as a task force and invite them to be catalysts for impact-engagement.

2. Convene the task force every month for six months to work through a series of increasingly substantial exercises that are designed to (a) clarify what we mean by impact and (b) begin to determine how we might see the effects of impact in those we serve.

3. After each exercise, commission every task force member to go out and meet with another group of key leaders within his or her department, division, branch, or area and take this new group through the same exercises each member has experienced in the task force, multiplying the engagement throughout the association.

4. Reconvene after each double-session to capture and communicate what we are learning about impact and how staff, members, partners, and constituencies are making meaning of the ideas and applying the evaluations.

5. After six months, design a collaborative means to keep people thinking about impact and evaluating and communicating the collective impact of the YMCA Calgary to staff, members, and stakeholders.

We lean back and look at our plan. It doesn't look like much. I think we imagine the afternoon might offer up something a bit more impressive. This plan is simple and low-tech. But sometimes simple and low-tech is most valuable when your aim is to engage people quickly and broadly. We have to find a way to help people interpret, adopt, and apply ideas of impact both personally and collectively. Meaning-making is not a given. It doesn't just happen, even with great ideas. It usually has to be modeled and prompted by others. Space has to be cleared for people to stop and reflect well. The core feature of our strategy is this: give a cadre of key leaders a reason to lead a series of structured conversations throughout the association, and through those conversations begin to shape a culture of impact. We want to foster widespread ownership of the ideas by having groups of people talk together and apply the ideas iteratively, purposefully, and over time. This is but one way to think about involving people, rather than simply telling them about impact and hoping the ideas stick.

Outcomes

To mature the notion of impact further, we need to unpack our ideas of intended impact into outcomes. For instance, if we, like the YMCA Calgary, were seeking to help people grow, thrive, lead, and belong, we would need to know more precisely what we mean by those words and what specific parts of growing, thriving, leading, and belonging we intend to effect. We wouldn't be able to tackle everything (no organization is *that* good), so we would determine what elements of these ideas would be our unique and particular focus.

Simply put, outcomes are the ideas' definitions. To keep the idea from being defined by chance, and to keep us from taking whichever parts of the definition happen to suit us in the moment, we crack open the idea, unpack it, and outline the primary pieces we intend to affect. For instance, if we say that we are helping people to lead, we will need to say also that these are the four or five (or more) components of leading that we aim to develop in people. If we set out to cause people to thrive, we have to say what about thriving we aim to influence. We need to choose carefully. These are our outcomes.

The idea of outcomes has emerged as a point of emphasis in recent years as organizations have sought to become more cause-driven. Accrediting councils, business strategists, nonprofit bodies, management consultants and educators alike have pushed us to think more clearly about developing strategy through outcomes. The downbeat of their message is this: Well-defined outcomes focus a group's efforts more strategically than well-tuned outputs. They keep the organizational gaze fixed on the purpose, the point, the cause of the work, and not simply the activity of the work. This makes the work more meaningful, more responsive to needs, more engaging to people, and more effective at moving the icebergs of human systems.

Outputs are what we do, provide, give, program, activate, offer, execute. *Outcomes* are what we hope to achieve with all of our activity. Outputs focus on us; outcomes on impact in others. Outputs are our production; outcomes are our effect. The shift in thinking from outputs to outcomes may seem small and hardly worth making, but the ramifications of conflating outputs and outcomes are profound. When outputs are taken for outcomes, an organization will measure its own effort and then claim that the sum of the effort equals effectiveness. It sounds like this: "We have provided services for X number of people" or "We have offered two additional service lines," or "We have three more departments that educate this many more people;" therefore, "We are effective!" The problem is in assuming our actions ensure an effect. We have to ask ourselves, what is all of this in service to?

The phrase, *in service to*, is a helpful Box C—*Intended Impact* designator, just as *in all things* demarcates Box A—*Ultimate Aims*. To get to the essence of Box C—*Intended Impact*, we need to ask persistently, "What is all of this *in service to?*" The new venture we are considering adopting? What is it *in service to?* The sum of our initiatives? What is *it in service to?* The balls each of us are juggling? What are they *in service to?* If we don't ask this question, a creeping Box E—*Action* will begin to swallow our attention and we will fill our days with more activity than intentionality. When we pay attention to what our work is *in service to*, we clarify our intent and strengthen our influence.

An outcome is a result. It's an achievement of impact, not an achievement of effort. Both are achievements. But the power of a mid-level Box C—*Intended Impact* outcome is that it keeps the main thing the main thing. It places our gaze squarely on the difference we are making in the *target* of the organization's mission—a group of people, a culture, client base, industry, and so forth. Box C—*Intended Impact* helps us resist the giant force pulling on our attention, prying our eyes off of others and onto ourselves, making us the central point. Besides, outputs are much easier to corner and count, pick apart and put back together. They are easier to see because they are right in front of us. But a marksman doesn't watch his rifle; he watches the target. A ballerina doesn't look down at her body; she looks up at a twirling horizon. A surfer doesn't stare at his surfboard; he pays attention to the destination the wave is curling him toward. Position, control, and technique are essentials, but only after we have gained a primary focus. When we watch the horizon of our effect in others for Box C—*Intended Impact*, we gain an important iceberg-moving poise and posture.

Since our subjects are human beings, those both within our organizations and through our organizations as clients and communities, our outcomes should be primarily about people and not inanimate notions. It's tempting to design outcomes for things like our work environment or company culture or community vitality, but a change of environment or culture or vitality is primarily a result of a change in people. We need to think about human change first. Our primary outcomes are people outcomes.

When we focus on people outcomes however, we have to grapple with a number of philosophical issues: How much can or should we impose our agenda on others? What values should shape our notion of intended impact? What is the fundamental nature of human beings anyway? These fascinating but thorny issues point to one reason why Box A—*Ultimate Aims* and Box B—*Core Convictions* need to precede the work of Box C—*Intended Impact.* Our own values have to be worked out before we can be clear in defining our intention for others.

As we think about our statements of outcome for people, it is helpful to differentiate what we can observe about people (their exterior features like behaviors, words, and feelings) from what is deeper within people (their interior features like beliefs, values, and devotion). The observable aspects are open to measurement. We can count changes in behavior, in what people report they have learned, and in the relative intensity of their feelings. We can assign numbers and scales to those elements of people and map their progress and trajectory. However, the deeper and more durable features, those elements closer to the human core and the metaphorical "heart" of a person, cannot be measured in the normal sense of measurement by counting, but they can still be credibly evaluated using a qualitative approach. Both kinds of outcomes are worth articulating.

Notice the difference in the following illustration of outcomes for Project Impact, and consider how you would frame an external and internal outcome for those you serve.

Outcome for the Exterior	Outcome for the Exterior
A cadre of management staff will • know fundamentals of qualitative research as applied to organizational contexts, • feel excited to inquire into qualities of human development, and • do research by completing three inquiries that exhibit technical competence.	A cadre of management staff will • believe in the value of human inquiry, • love exploring why people are as they are, and • become connoisseurs of human growth and development in organizations.

Indicators

How do we know we are making progress on our outcomes? Indicators will tell us. For this we need both measures and tell-tale signs.

Measures indicate the progress on the exterior outcomes of people. They enumerate the components of an exterior outcome, broken down, teased apart into portions, and sequenced. They are often framed in numeric terms—as things you can observe and count. For example, satisfaction rates among credit union members will be increased by 10 percent this year in order to advance the lender's vision for a vibrant economy in a local community. Or, an employee will need to obtain a 70 percent level of proficiency on a scale of skills by the end of the first module in order to attain an outcome of expertise. Or, the seniors in a community will need to exhibit statistically significant progress along an array of core civic competencies within five years to fulfill the outcome of a healthy and vital aging population. Most outcomes of significance cannot be swallowed in one bite. We need indicators to keep us from choking on the big idea of impact.

Outcomes for the exterior need measures to show progress on the external parts of people. But what about outcomes for the interior? If we desire outcomes that have more to do with the *quality* of human achievement—human growth and development, belief change and maturation, shared values and ethos within people at a corporation, group momentum and the like—measures will be useless. Measures are only good to break down outcomes that can be pieced apart and enumerated. Qualitative outcomes defy division. In fact, many of the best and most powerful elements of Box C—*Intended Impact* cannot be dissected precisely because they have to do with indivisible elements of human development. We care deeply about those outcomes as well, and that is why we need *tell-tale signs*.

Tell-tale signs are the immaterial, immeasurable, and sometimes ineffable portions of a Box C—*Intended Impact*. They are, in fact, essential for any organization focused on people, for they illuminate and affirm the depth and not just the breadth of the work, the qualities and not just the quantities, the subtleties and nuances, not simply the overt and obvious. In fact, we need to talk about tell-tale signs to keep everyone's focus on the important things that can't quite be locked into concrete, numeric terms but are nonetheless essential to the purpose.

What are the tell-tale signs that we are having a deeper kind of impact in people? What are the immeasurable indicators of success in the immeasurably important outcomes of human impact? We may find that tell-tale signs best come in symbolic or metaphoric form. Having clarity about this picture (or pictures) helps us define what we truly want to see happen, regardless of whether it can be measured quantitatively. We tend to shy away from defining indicators qualitatively because we assume what cannot be measured cannot be evaluated. But qualities, even though they cannot be reduced to numbers, are still empirical. They can be accessed through a different kind of data. Given a qualitative technique, we can credibly assess tell-tale signs as well.

Articulating tell-tale signs affirms the value of the qualities that lie at the heart of organizational intent and remind people to pay attention to those difficult-to-define attributes. When working with people, tell-tale signs should accompany measures. Here are various examples of each—measures and tell-tale signs. Notice the concrete and precise nature of measures and the symbolic and metaphoric nature of the tell-tale signs:

Measures for the Exterior	Tell-tale Signs for the Interior
• Staff engagement ratings will increase by 10%. • Each participating manager will renovate one signature program according to our revised standards within the next 6 months. • Stakeholder contributions will grow by 7% annually.	There will be among our employees • a buzz of re-energized purpose among managers, • a groundswell of belonging and *esprit de corps,* • a re-awakening of people and leaning-in to the meaning of their work.

Envisioning impact

I imagine that all of this Box C maneuvering may seem like over-thinking and over-working the fairly straightforward concept of intentionality. But I'm not so sure the concept of intentionality is straightforward most of the time. Many of us wrestle to make this clear. Take your personal life, for example. What kind of impact would you like to make on the world? These ideas will certainly evolve over time, but right now, what is your clearest sense for the unique contribution you intend to have, and how do you envision people to be different because you've been here, giving your life to what you are giving it?

For practice, take out a piece of paper and draft a personal Box C—*Intended Impact.* Write down the key ideas of your essential impact and unpack the points of outcome that would be your effect on your family and friends, your community and profession. Then, to mature the ideas further, imagine what might be the measures and tell-tale signs that you were achieving this dream of impact. You may be surprised at the clarity that Box C—*Intended Impact* work provides. A solid sense of a personal intended impact, when there is congruence between work and life, increases capacity for both. There is quite a bit of talk about work-life balance these days. An exercise like this holds power to achieve for us work-life coherence, not just balance.

You've heard it said, "If you aim at nothing, you'll hit it every time." That might be an overstatement, as proverbs tend to be, for we can never anticipate every impact with prescient aim. We will undoubtedly be surprised at times by some effects we could never foresee, even on our most well-aimed days. We will accomplish things through our work with others that we could never plan or prepare for—great things, wonderful things. Some of these will happen simply because our Box A—*Ultimate Aims* and Box B—*Premises* are sound and resonant and animating our essence. Still, we need to aim well. Some of the inadvertent and unexpected effects of our lives and work, some of our most fortuitous and providential outcomes of impact, will appear only because we are heading in a direction, and only because we are gripped by an idea of what difference we intend to make in the people we are here to serve. They will be because we have a clear and compelling Box C. This is the power of *Intended Impact*.

Hints for Developing Box C
Intended Impact

1. Focus firmly on impact instead of effort for Box C. Resist placing goals for your own performance in this box—items of output (for example, number of offerings, levels of efficiency, growth in services, etc.). Instead, define the difference in others you intend to nudge into reality.

2. Remember that ideas of impact are good only if they are used. Use the three criteria of high-level ideas of *Intended Impact* to vet your words and phrases—sticky, resonant, generative. They don't need to be fancy, just make sure they are memorable and meaningful.

3. Explore the rival and less resonant ideas that take up residence in Box C and affect your steerage. Develop a strategy to keep those encroaching ideas from compromising your focus.

4. Include qualitative outcomes, not just quantitative outcomes. Some of the best ideas about impact will be immeasurable.

5. Develop multiple editions of Box C. It usually takes a few iterations before the ideas of Box C mature. Keep at it.

6. Involve others throughout your organization (and even key partners) in the development of Box C thinking. Remember to engage people deeply enough that they feel ownership over the ideas so that they become a living and driving force for them too.

6. BEST MEANS: BOX D

Tinker Hatfield heads product design at Nike, Inc. and holds the title of Vice President of Innovation. In the expansive industry of athletic apparel he is both elder-statesman and guru of design. Years ago, while Hatfield was still an unknown architectural undergraduate student, running track at the University of Oregon, he was recruited by coach Bill Bowerman to turn laps while wearing shoes studded with experimental waffle-like nobs of rubber. The sketches Hatfield drew after stretching his feet in Bowerman's inventive platforms became the early prototypes for what has become one of the world's most revered athletic companies.

For the past 30 years, Hatfield has created many of Nike's signature products, including the renowned Air Jordan, and has recruited some of its most prodigious athletes. Aside from products and partnerships, he has helped to shape a strong and unique company culture: the style, ethos, and attitude of Nike employees, particularly the designers, are sharply recognizable. There is a restless, innovative edge and irrepressible, creative drive to them. They seem to have a unique knack for designing iconic shoes that draw people in. Decades after the release of the first Air Jordan, kids still stand in line waiting for each new release.

It is an icy afternoon in December and I am making my way to the Nike headquarters in Beaverton, Oregon to ask Hatfield what he thinks about developing people. His office sits on the ground floor of the Mia Hamm building, tucked in the corner of the expansive and imaginative room aptly dubbed the "innovation kitchen." The capacious space is filled with drawings and products in various stages of development along with pictures and pieces from the past, relics of the company's storied history. It is open, untidy, stimulating. It's as if the overflow of evolutionary activity crammed its creative particles into one bulging place. A group of brainy creative types sit conspiring at a bar-height table. A Nike veteran, his head touched with gray, saunters through, bantering with designers along the way before disappearing through a back door. And then, at one edge of the space, Hatfield turns away from an animated conversation and rolls his chair over to the curved, modern sofa where I sit to describe what makes their means, their Box D, unique.

"Every product tells a story," he explains. "That's what makes it authentic, for us and for those who use it. And that's what connects our story to the story of others. A human story infuses each one of our products with meaning." I soon discover that in the design rooms of Nike, every new athletic shoe line embodies an attribute, experience, or achievement of an athlete, or of the design process that created it. Every piece of apparel is intended to correlate to the human narrative and represent the larger story of human life. Engaging the story of the human experience is central to their approach of product design.

"Sport is a universal and global experience," says Hatfield. "People of every culture and ethnicity know about winning and losing, about trying your best and getting better, about striving and reaching for some great achievement, about sometimes failing and then getting up to try again. Our style is to tap those stories. We want to tell the story of human experience through our products." This is the "Nike way." It might look like simply telling a story, but it is more than that. It is engaging the human narrative and connecting with the life experience of people. That every Nike design should interact with the human story is a potent part of their Box D — *Best Means*. And as a Box D—*Best Means,* it characterizes and infuses and modifies the unique way the designers at Nike approach each other and their craft. This is the work of Box D—*Best Means.*

The idea of best means

In our ideological iceberg, Box D holds *Best Means*—the principles on which we base the methodologies and strategies we use to accomplish our purpose. A means is a way. It is the process through which we believe people best grow and develop. If we were to answer the following questions using principles—not practices—we would get right to the heart of Box D: What kinds of interventions best make progress toward our intended impact? What are the best ways to help people and groups of people develop? What characterizes the most catalytic interactions we can have with others?

When we ask leaders about means, we often get answers about what is general, standard, average, and commonly happening day after day, month after month, year after year. "This," they say, "is what we usually do and how we generally approach things around here." An average is a mathematical notion. It's a norm. Thinking about a means as an average is an idea that has jumped the species, crossing from mathematical parlance and into organizational dialogue. But we intend something different than the norm for Box D—*Best Means;* we envision an articulation of the principles informing and governing our best strategies.

Another way people speak about means is to use the popular language of "best practices." Means, in this case, are noted industry exemplars and noteworthy performances. These are top of the class, best in show, high-water marks, shining stars, state-of-the-art achievements. They are the cases we lift up for emulation—the best of the best. When we are asked about the means of work, then, we often hear about our best performances: "Let me tell you about our best work or what our star employee or stellar program has accomplished. Let me show you what we can do when we are really on our game." The best case is good to know and emulate, but it is not Box D—*Best Means.* *Best Means* are the reasons why the best practices are best. They are characteristics or principles, not practices.

Both of these—general statements of average and specific illustrations of best practice—represent what is true about a person or an organization, but neither should fill Box D—*Best Means.* Instead, we place in Box D the reasons why we choose particular plans above others, the commitments causing us to adopt certain strategies instead of others, and what we believe needs to characterize everything we do to achieve the greatest impact. We use Box D—*Best Means* to get clear about the values that inform what we do—values about engagement, process, methodology, intervention, and advocacy.

As with the designers at Nike, a good Box D—*Best Means* explains how high-performing teams exhibit a strong sense of strategic coherence: they are driven by common principles about the characteristics of preferred methodology. Box Ds provide a strategy screen, a kind of rubric to help vet choices, so that teams can make congruent and clearheaded decisions on the ground. These ideas help teams stay faithful to the theory of engagement and refrain from defaulting to the most common or convenient path. They give teams a way to resist the allure of pure pragmatism or raw opportunity when faced with options contrary to their philosophy. They offer a chance to be intentional about what kind of ideas should drive and animate any and all action.

For the designers at Nike, engaging the human story is the best way to design products, serve people, and grow a company. They believe that the human story of dedication, competition, endurance, and achievement, and what sports represent, is the point at which products and people meaningfully intersect. It's a clear Box D — *Best*

Means. And, like most good Box D—*Best Means* precepts, it permeates the culture of Nike and shapes their way of work. Hatfield says that a "constant drip" of story-telling permeates the organization and infuses Box E — *Action.* He gives me a few examples: The CEO regularly sends memos with stories to emphasize key organizational maxims. Dedicated story-tellers, veterans who know the organizational meanings, intentionally wander the halls and remind employees of core organizational narratives. Corporate thought-leaders constantly appeal to anecdotes new and old, from a professional athlete at the pinnacle of popularity to an obscure cancer survivor trying to recover strength through physical exercise. Hatfield also explains that as Nike gets better at engaging the human experiences through their products, more people connect their own stories to Nike and are drawn in.

Effects from Box D

An effective Box D—*Best Means* acts like an adverb to a verb; it modifies how the action happens. While Box E—*Action* explains what we do (the verb), Box D—*Best Means* (the adverb) prescribes how we do things and why we do them this way. Isolating, examining, and developing principles of how and why we do things certain ways provides three critical benefits. (1) *Selectivity:* we can choose one particular plan over another by reason and rationale. (2) *Innovation:* we can broaden our range of applications for any particular commitment. (3) *Style and coherence:* we can exhibit a recognizable and unique organizational or personal signature.

1. Saying no—Selectivity

Occasionally, when I have posed a question to a room filled with leaders, asking what they need most to lead more effectively, I hear a curious response. "We wish we knew what *not* to do!" they exclaim. At first, this sentiment sounds quite odd. "You want to know what, exactly? What not to do?" But after a moment's reflection it begins to make more sense. Given the array of opportunities facing any good leader, the ability to say a strategic "no" is as important as a "yes."

Disciplined choice-making is the crux of strategic management. With unlimited time and resources, anything and everything is possible. But given that one or both are limited, we must choose wisely between what we will adopt and what we will pass by. Without an apparatus to help us be selective, our mission gets swamped by hyperactivity, a frenzy that dilutes potency and distracts us from our vision. Good ideas, even great ideas, sometimes need to be turned down. How do we refuse a good idea on grounds more sufficient than simply because we are over-loaded or over-extended? Without a way to vet ideas for congruence and philosophical soundness we will not be able to make these decisions wisely. Our Box D—*Best Means* can help us, but only if we think carefully about what inhabits this part of our ideological iceberg.

Consider how Tanis Cochrane and her team at the Calgary YMCA shaped a way forward for the work of Box C—*Intended Impact*. They were quick to identify a number of options for Box E—*Action*. That wasn't hard. One of the most alluring possibilities was to hire a consulting group specializing in survey work related to impact. However, they hold in their Box D—*Best Means* a commitment to *true engagement* among staff and constituencies. An external firm, they recognized, would give them technical expertise, but not ownership. Engagement, for them, means more than informing, more than even involving. It means developing in people the capacity to see and shape intended impact together. This best means idea helps them say no to the external project as the centerpiece (although they will use still use it to augment their work and provide key points of credibility) and instead design a project that truly engages their staff, members, and community partners and develops their capacity to see for themselves and tell the story of their collective impact with credibility.

As you might imagine, stuffing our Box D—*Best Means* with any *good* means is insufficient. We have to be philosophically selective. What do we believe makes one means better than another? What does our philosophy of engagement say about the characteristics of our most potent strategies as opposed to other options? We cannot simply be responsible eclectics, picking and choosing in the moment, or we will become overcome by the most urgent or alluring. We need clear ideas of best means to guide us. Some of these ideas will come from our core convictions in Box B. Others will come from evidence and the research-base of our sector. Still others will come from our analysis of the formative characteristics embedded in best practices from the field. The real work of Box D is to pay attention to the best part of best means.

A simple exercise might be helpful: Take each nomination for Box D—*Best Means* and contrast this idea with what it might be confused with in the minds of colleagues or others. If someone hears the idea second-hand, what might they mistake you for meaning? Force yourself to distinguish between what you mean and what others might think you mean by the idea. This requires getting explicit about the values underlying your thinking. Whether you agree with the following statements, take the exercise as an example:

What we mean	What we don't mean
Disequilibration is the best engine for human growth and development.	• Too much challenge = traumatizing • Too little challenge = over-contextualizing • One brief moment of challenge • Single-sized challenge fits all, etc.
Building intentional relationships and partnerships best catalyzes impact.	• Collaboration should be attained at any cost • Partners need not have congruence with our values • The more partners, the better, etc.
The act of interpretation best helps people grasp and more deeply attach to the mission.	• People can impose whatever interpretation they want on the work • Telling people what to believe • Awkward or pejorative moments of meaning-making, etc.

2. Developing new strategies—Innovation

Have you ever wondered at the speed with which programs become sacrosanct, unable to be questioned or reconsidered? Have you ever noticed how quickly we become married to certain programs or practices and forget the principles driving them? This happens when Boxes D and E become inadvertently fused in our minds. It's a failure to keep a distinction between the principles of our best means (Box D) and the exemplars of our best practices (Box E). We can't innovate without losing who we are because we are what we have been doing. Our only way forward is to get better at what we do. When we separate Box D—*Best Means* from Box E—*Action* however, we can experiment with new actions while maintaining our organizational integrity;

we liberate our organizational identity from the specifics of our programs. The result is to embolden innovation. `

Without the Box D-E distinction, we conflate *who we are* with *what we do,* so we can't evolve programmatically without an identity crisis. Also, when we define ourselves primarily by Box E — *Action* instead of Box D—*Best Means,* we tend to grow by finding something that works and then replicating the form over and over. We make copies of the original. And the quality of these copies, no matter how hard we try, usually diminishes as the distance from the initial source grows, just like the copies from the old mimeograph machines we used during my childhood would become increasingly blurry with usage. When a group defines itself primarily by a Box E — *Action,* its dexterity and spontaneity and adaptability stiffen into arthritic restraint. People fear that if they let go of what they do, they will be letting go of who they are. A healthy Box D—*Best Means* allows us to experiment with new actions without threatening the basic culture and values and essence of the organization.

A well-articulated Box D—*Best Means* is thus more liberating than constraining. Many who go through this process of developing an ideology fear that a strong Box D might limit options, inhibit experimentation, and stifle creativity. They find, however, that Box D works in a counter-intuitive sense: it actually encourages the kind of innovation that is congruent with the philosophical DNA of the organization. With a health and robust Box D, we are free to develop new and fresh practices and release a cascade of creative energy while retaining our organizational DNA. Here's how it works:

⋯⟩ If we designate a best means such as, "people learn best when they are meaningfully connected and engaged with others," we may find its Box E — *Action* expressed in many different ways—a mentoring program, learning triads, collaborative vision sessions, or something we have yet to think of. We can innovate broadly, but congruently.

⋯⟩ If we adopt a Box D like, "organizations develop best when they are grown according to biological models instead of mechanistic ones," we will prepare nurturing environments and protect the time it will take for new initiatives to take root and bear fruit, redesign leadership training to be more about DNA and less about compliance, attend to the diversity of our organizational eco-system, and set the conditions for true multiplication instead of just franchising. We may try a variety of actions, but make sure the new experiments align with our core philosophy of development.

⋯⟩ If we are convinced that both employees and consumers engage best when they experience and identify with the human story within us, then we, like Nike, will enfold a deliberate interaction with the human narrative into our design, marketing, leadership, and organizational ethos.

A solid Box D opens the door to creativity and innovation while simultaneously strengthening unity, integrity, and congruence among every initiative and everyone involved.

3. Gaining a distinctive way—Style and Coherence

A healthy Box D will not only clarify decision-making and bolster innovation, it will also reveal a sense of style. Think about style for a moment. What is style, and how do you know it when you see it? A thoughtful coordination of clothes, accessories, attitude, and bearing—and a person has style. Rarely do we see someone thoughtlessly disheveled and say that he or she has style (unless, of course, that person is sporting the carefully crafted, un-crafted look—that too is style of a different kind).

Style is a function of intentionality, whether it's adornment, behavior, or attitude. It is the distinctive characteristics of how we look or act. It is the antithesis of merely throwing on whatever is most convenient from the morning's closet or acting like everyone else in the moment, whether personally or organizationally. Style takes some deliberation and forethought. It is a commitment. A thoughtful Box D—*Best Means* will provide a person or an institution with the stuff of style. Engaging people in the human story has become part of the Nike style, the "Nike way." When someone says that you or your organization has a way, it is your Box D—*Best Means* they are talking about. For a moment, consider what others might say of your Box D—*Best Means*. What is your way? What would those who experience your organization say is your *style*?

A clear Box D—*Best Means* also secures an elegant coherence and meaningful integrity to our work. The word "integrity" comes from the Latin, integritas, from which we also get word integer, the "whole" number. It has to do with the unity among the pieces of any person or organization. A good Box D holds the individual pieces of strategy together in a congruent, complementary, connected whole. When this box is sound and the ideas embedded broadly in staff or employees, there is a common sense throughout an organization, consistent across departments and levels, no matter how varied the actual tactics may be.

Notice how the statements of Box D for the Bill and Melinda Gates Foundation give stylistic coherence to over $25 billion in grant making activities throughout more than 100 countries:

⋯⟩ We identify a specific point of intervention and apply our efforts against a theory of change.

⋯⟩ We take risks, make big bets, and move with urgency. We are in it for the long haul.

⋯⟩ We advocate—vigorously but responsibly—in our areas of focus.

⋯⟩ We must be humble and mindful in our actions and words.

⋯⟩ We seek and heed the counsel of outside voices.

⋯⟩ We treat our grantees as valued partners, and we treat the ultimate beneficiaries of our work with respect.

It's as if the Gates foundation is orchestrating a massive symphony of charitable activity, and their Box D is acting like a key signature for the musical score. In music, the key is the primary code for how to interpret the notes on the sheet. It dictates how those notes will be played. The key of B-flat, for instance, stipulates that B-flat and an E-flat must be played throughout the score to provide melodic coherence. There may be occasions when a composer uses accidentals (an E-flat goes to E-natural to cause some momentary effect) or creates movements in a larger piece (the entire key changes, say to C-major, for a longer span and then back again to add texture and intrigue and depth). In either case, the best ways to play notes may be suspended for a time to accomplish a certain change in overall tone, but the primary *feel* of the piece will follow a consistent code.

Effective leaders of iceberg-moving organizations, like composers, develop a "key signature" that dictates how the notes will be played. They may choose to respond to particular situations or challenges with a temporal accidental or key change. But most use a primary set of Box D—*Best Means* commitments over and over again. The more fully a team is imbued with these commitments and the more naturally they follow them, the better the harmony. For each of us, having Box D—*Best Means* commitments about how to proceed, how to engage, and how to develop strategy will guide not only what we should and should not do, but just as significantly, how we should and should not do it.

How to develop a Box D

When developing a Box D—*Best Means*, the place to look first is our Box B—*Core Convictions*. Both boxes carry beliefs. Both are frequently overlooked and yet hold brilliance for informing organizational leadership and development. Both dictate the signature DNA of any group. The difference between B and D is this: Box B contains beliefs about reality; Box D holds implications of those beliefs for the way forward. Take the following as examples:

⋯> Box B: People need purpose in their lives.

Box D: Hence, we grow our staff and clients best when we engage them in meaning-making and point them to a higher good.

⋯> Box B: Human beings are mind, body, and spirit.

Box D: Hence, we develop them best through integration (helping them see connections) and praxis (pushing theory to action and action to reflection).

⋯> Box B: We each have a dark side.

Box D: Hence, we all need the perspectives and accountability of trusted others in order to mature and develop best.

In addition to thinking through implications of Box B—*Core Convictions* for our Box D—*Best Means,* it is helpful to examine the research in our sector. Disciplining ourselves to seek scholarship keeps us from promulgating *cherished theories* about best means. All of us, and all of our organizations, become attached at some point to misguided, malformed, or erroneous cherished theories about how things work best. Many of these are tough to shake because they have become so deeply ingrained in thinking over time. They are organizational assumptions, ideas about how things best work that we don't question. Our cherished theories come from corporate legends, our own experiences (which are often less representative than we imagine), and the assumptive pronouncements made by people we respect. It is essential to keep reading credible research in order to debunk cherished theories and enlighten us to true best means. Research is a rich resource for Box D—Best Means.

It is also helpful to look to best practices, anecdotes, and our own autobiographies to inform the development of our Box D—*Best Means.* We have to be careful when using these, however. The critical function of best practices, anecdotes, and our autobiographies is to act heuristically and illuminate the principles behind what seems to have worked well. These are technically Box E—*Actions,* but they often give us clues to underlying characteristics about Box D—*Best Means* theories of change. The principle part (instead of the practice part) of a theory of change helps us craft best means. To get there, we ask questions like, "What makes that best practice best? What principle does that example illustrate? Why was that personal experience or encounter so rich, meaningful, and powerful?" In so asking, we start to peel away the practice and get deeper into the Box D—*Best Means*.

With a robust and meaningful Box D—*Best Means*, we can then turn to action and begin to pull on the levers of iceberg-moving change and design our Box E—*Action*.

Hints for Developing Box D
Best Means

1. Use the implications of Box B—*Core Convictions* to populate Box D – *Best Means*. A thoughtful rehearsal of B will enrich D.

2. Resist the temptation to place "best practices" in Box D. Instead look for the principles embedded in the practice. Best Means is about "best choices," the reasons to favor certain practices over others.

3. Be sure to use the research relevant to your notions of best means. Rather than simply filling Box D with preferences, strive to draw from a well of social science. An evidence-based Box D is a powerful Box D.

4. Use the exercise specifying what "we mean" and what "we don't mean" to help clarify the essentials and avoid confusion.

5. Explore the possibility that some current best means are incongruent with desired best means. Taking a candid look at the common denominators in existing practices will illuminate current reality.

6. Aim for a few ideas that can be broadly applied. As with the other boxes, the ideas can only be used widely if they are memorable and meaningful.

7. Action: Box E

I t was the mid-1990s, and I had just accepted a teaching job at a small, private university. I was right out of graduate school, eager to change the world but conscious that I already had many habits and predilections both good and bad, ruts in my own Box E—*Action*. For a few years before going to graduate school I led community programs for youth and had accumulating a number of experiences teaching young people in non-formal contexts. The work came rather naturally. It hadn't taken me long to figure out how to interact with adolescents. Since I was only a few years older than most of them, I leaned heavily on personal rapport and charisma. But after receiving an invitation to join the faculty of an institution of higher education, I knew I needed a better strategy to shoulder this more weighty teaching challenge.

I was a young and idealistic professor, eager to shape the minds of these students and impact their ways of thinking. I had endured enough mind-numbing lectures from professors during my own education to know that I would try just about anything to avoid inuring these students with a semester full of dry soliloquys. I had also been radically undone and re-done by other magnificently persuasive professors who changed my life for good. The latter had touched me with the power and possibility of good teaching. But my practice had been forged in a community context with teenagers, not in the university classroom. I suspected it would take something more than personality or affability and something different than a newly-titled Ph.D.'s head spewing course content. But what about my old habits?

If I was going to force myself into a better practice—practice more in line with my philosophy of learning—I would need to think carefully about my own Boxes and then apply myself diligently to them. I decided to post five words on the wall above my desk about my Box D—*Best Means*. Just five. Five ideas about a theory of learning, affixed to the wall in front of me. I didn't think I would be able to handle more. I used Box D—*Best Means* because it represented some of the best of my A, B, and C positions. So I forced myself to choose the best five ideas I could. The choosing turned out to be the easy part. Every day for most of that first year, with every new lesson plan and before I left my office to step into the classroom, I checked my plan (Box E) against my beliefs about what makes people learn best (Box D).

I wish I could say that my practice quickly came in line with my ideology, but it was much more challenging than that. As it turns out, my personal iceberg doesn't move very easily. (I expect my friends and family have probably known this about me for some time now.) Even this simple exercise of praxis—bringing theory to life in practice— took more work and courage than I imagined. At times it felt excruciating, like learning how to walk anew. Time and again I returned to fix my teaching plan, rework it, rethink the implication of my commitments, and press my philosophy into my practice. The pace of change was glacial at first. I could hardly believe how much time and work it was taking to mold myself to my ideology. Only in time and after much effort did it begin to go more smoothly. I started to see what my beliefs look like in action. After a year or two I began to develop a feel for the practice. And then, finally, there it was: evidence of iceberg-turning impact in students. But those first steps, breaking out of old ruts came slowly, deliberately, painfully.

An ideology is mere theory until it begins to change our behavior.

The human iceberg is moved when the ideology is pressed into action, when Box E—*Action* becomes resonant with the meanings of intentionality and, in turn, authenticates the ideology. All the right thinking in the world cannot change any of us until it starts affecting our day-by-day, hour-by-hour ways of living. Getting ideas to gain traction in practice sometimes means taking determined steps out of deep ruts. It may mean posting a few beliefs on a wall and not walking out the door until there are some clear steps of iceberg application.

That which moves us

The question we have been wrestling with throughout this entire discussion is this: What makes one action, intervention, program, initiative, or engagement more powerful than any other to truly make a transformative change in people? Which kind of Box E — *Action* moves an iceberg and which just chips away at its surface? How can we increase the odds that our lives and our organizations will have the kind of lasting impact we desire?

We have been rehearsing this key idea time and again: The most potent Box E — *Action* is both formed and nourished by vibrant renditions of Boxes A, B, C, and D and engages the human system we intend to change in its Boxes A, B, C, and D. Simply put, effective above-the-surface programs are expressions of sound below-the-surface positions. They also intervene in below-the-surface positions of others. They are not just actions done with flair and flourish; they are deep, meaningful, and moving.

Let's return to a few of our examples and see how they handle Box E tip-of-the-iceberg issues with below-the-surface strategies.

At the University of Monaco, Boris Porkovich and Maxime Crener have innumerable tactical possibilities they could employ to secure change in the business mind-set of emerging graduates, and through them to the business milieu of the region. But to make a durable difference, they realize they can't just add a couple of initiatives. Any "add-on" program—a class, retreat, or even academic track—might just skip off the surface of people. Their real task is to embed their deeper convictions into the culture of their institution and deliberately develop the deeper convictions of their students, not just teach them skills.

Consequently, they are initiating a broader series of conversations within the university community about what kind of education matters most for making a change in the ethos of global business practice. A conversation may not seem like much of an action (and this is merely their first step), but it can be powerful if it is the right kind of conversation. David Cooperrider from Case Western Reserve University claims that every organization grows in the direction of its most persistent inquiries. If he is right, then certain kinds of conversations can be creatively disruptive, strategically formative, and useful for transforming the underlying values within people. Their plan of action is a deliberate attempt to start leveraging what is below the surface.

Sergey Rakhuba and his team are enjoying the acclaim School Without Walls is receiving. The model of ministerial preparation works so well throughout the regions of the former Soviet Union that word is getting out. Now, religious leaders from Belarus to Moldova are asking permission to adopt the model. School Without Walls is facing the challenge of spread. But how do you multiply a program without jeopardizing its core principles and, in so doing, compromising its iceberg-moving power?

It would be tempting to write a manual on the *School Without Walls* program (Box E) and then franchise the operation. They have the programmatic kinks worked out, so why not simply license the model and train people for compliance? If they took such a course of replicating practice, they would simply be passing along Box E—*Action* absent the part of the iceberg under the water, the values and positions making it work so well. The hazard is the classic danger of going to scale for any successful program: promulgating the form instead of the substance. To engage below the surface, they have decided that their first step is to publish a primer about the underlying beliefs, values, positions, and strategies that inform and secure School Without Walls. Then they will hold forums, not primarily to train in the model and disseminate the curriculum, but to engage with others about the guiding ideas driving School Without Walls.

Since the opening of the Robert Lee YMCA in Vancouver, Simon Adams and his staff have been overwhelmed by the public's ebullient response. Memberships have exceeded all forecasts. In a few short months, their numbers are fully a year ahead of expectations. The downtown community and its civic leaders have lauded the restored, state-of-the-art presence of the YMCA in the pulsing heart of the city. Management could easily be seduced into assuming that iceberg-moving is happening just because there is a flurry of activity, a rousing ring of support, and a bulging sheet of financials. Adams and his team realize, however, that the positive press about their new, gleaming tower might actually undermine the potency of their difference-making. The rush of popularity might distract them and cause them to fail to consciously embody their philosophy of human engagement. And so, they are deliberately returning to animate their staff with the ideas in their Boxes so that deeper change in their members and the community might be stirred.

Dr. Ruth Weibe and her administrative team in School District 33 had the option of leveraging the merger of three departments into one through superficial means. They could have relied on the social pressure of relocating everyone into one physical space, a new administrative building. They could have trusted in policies to dictate alignment. They could have banked on evaluation metrics and the big stick of performance reviews to ensure compliance. They took all of these actions. But in addition, and concurrently, they decided to convene a series of day-long meetings, once a month for almost a year, to develop a shared ideology. The dialogue about Boxes A, B, C, and D forces a quality of interaction about the guiding assumptions, values, and philosophy of each department, and how they need to develop a unity (not uniformity) of thinking if they are to have a unified and forceful presence within their community.

These are examples of iceberg-moving action. They are each different, but they hold this in common: they intentionally seek to leverage the ideology below the waterline to promote change and development in people. They eschew practice disconnected from theory. They deliberately dive into the depths of what people believe to move the iceberg from a deeper point of leverage. They don't rely on the external structure or re-structure to change things but instead invest in the people whose presence will be the primary shaping force for the future. Herein lies the task of Box E—*Action:* holding our practices to the formative force of Boxes A, B, C, and D.

To review: When Box E disconnects from the rest of the iceberg, we focus on execution alone. Our conversation devolves to things like, "How did we perform?" "How can we execute better?" "How can we make sure there are fewer errors in what we do?" "How can we lock this down to ensure no variance or slip in quality?" "How can we squeeze more in?" These, and considerations like these, become the primary points of attention. When Box E is the primary box in view, or if it captures an inordinate proportion of our attention, there will first be an erosion of meaning and then a corrosion of practice. We may not see it right away, but in a matter of time performance fades, momentum slips, and we are back where we started. It's why advice-giving rarely changes reality, why inspirational speeches make little difference in the long-term, why platitudes render such insubstantial impressions, and why compliance keeps people secure but rarely inspires creativity, passion, and sacrifice. To be developed, people need more than to be told or even trained.

In the short run, focusing exclusively on our Box E—*Action* may serve us well. It can tighten sagging practices and fix dangling pieces. But over time, its over-emphasis makes it very difficult for us to inspire people, develop future visionary leadership, nurture creativity and nimbleness of thought, or promote depth of passion and understanding. When most of our energy goes to setting and shoring up practice, our perspective narrows into a tunnel of tactics. Our strategies sink to efficiencies. But when our Box E—*Action* is a true and authentic expression of our Ultimate Aims, Premises, Intended Impact, and Best Means, our Action can be tremendously and powerfully transformative.

The formative power of Box E

If we are being overly cautious right now about Box E—*Action,* it is to compensate for the way we often neglect the other Boxes. But we should remember that a strategic Box E—*Action* can be a wonderful tool of formation, even for the whole of the iceberg. In other words, even though we can't move an iceberg by simply pulling on the tip, we shouldn't ignore how the tip of the iceberg can be a catalyst for change in the position of the whole. Our Box E—*Action* can be a strikingly effective aid to the formation and development of the underlying ideology of ourselves and others. There are at least three significant ways that a well-formed Box E can have a truly catalytic effect. Let's use three metaphors to unpack these notions:

1. **Action as a tutor**. Sometimes people can experience a renovation in their hearts and a change in their minds and yet not know what those changes mean in actual, day-to-day practice. Here, a clear rendering of Box E—*Action* acts like a tutor. It specifies what it looks like to hold those new beliefs and values in concrete practice. It shapes understanding by demonstrating practice that is tied to understanding. At times in our development, each of us needs some specific tutoring in order to "get it." We need specific instruction on what it looks like, sounds like, and feels like. And we need someone to help us connect the dots between a belief and an action. Practice accompanied by meaning-making is a powerful catalyst for learning.

2. **Action as a mirror.** The people we serve occasionally think they have experienced a turning of their iceberg, when in fact only the tip has been rearranged. Their iceberg has been given only a makeover and so only the veneer has changed. They may have new labels, but the ideas are old. They may sound different, but the story is the same. A good Box E—*Action* will serve as a mirror in these situations, reflecting what is still true. When we prescribe a standard of action and that standard is not met, the gap is exposed. Specifying behaviors and their accompanying criteria (to what extent the behaviors are to be practiced) keeps people from being able to hide behind a smoke-screen of good words and good intentions. A set of specified actions, when placed in contrast to the current actions of one who claims to be changed, will often reveal the need for deeper and more genuine growth and development.

3. **Action as a cast.** A good Box E—*Action*, in a helahty way, can break malformed habits, just as an orthopedic surgeon will break malformed or misaligned bones. It forces a new way in us. Once a practice is reset, we need a cast to hold the practice in place while we re-develop strength in this new form. We need feedback loops to keep us in place. We need an ecternal apparatus, just like a cast, to hold us while we develop strength. A well-articulated Box E—*Action* performs this role, holding us to a new way of actiing from the outside while we develop the ability to hold ourselves to a new way from the inside.

Developing action

If you haven't done this yet, try forming a Box E, or at least part of a Box E, using your underlying Boxes. Start with some initial statements of Boxes A and B, then C and D. From there, press your positions into the action of Box E. Remember, the real power lies not in filling the boxes on paper, but in acting with congruence to what you believe. To diagram this, start from the base of the iceberg and work your way from Box A to Box E. See if there might be actions that are a clear expression of your ideology.

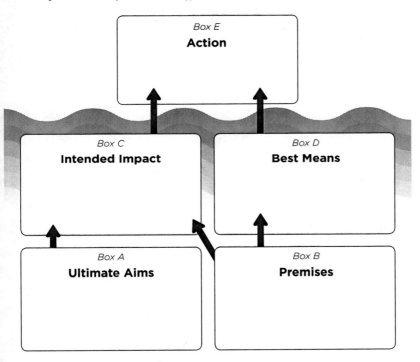

Diagnosing effectively

Using the Boxes in the direction of A to E helps develop and maintain intentionality in our difference-making efforts. We start at Box A—who we (or our organization) desire to be—and move up through the iceberg toward the surface. We articulate what ought to be the case. However, the Boxes can be used as a diagnostic tool as well, to discover the underlying causes of practices, behaviors, or circumstances. If we enter at Box E—what we are currently doing—and move down into the water of our iceberg to determine why the action is such action, we will illuminate what is the case below the surface.

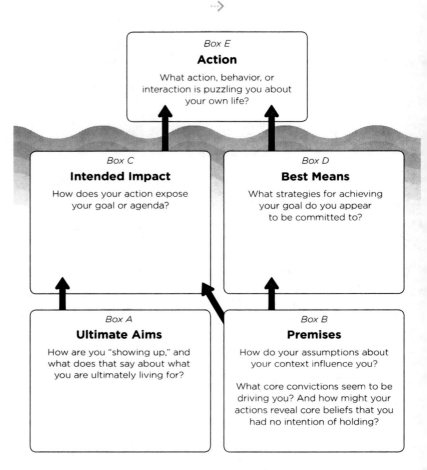

Box E is where the proof of our philosophical commitments lies. If we have a compelling Box A, B, C, and D, and they nourish Box E, we are poised to make a difference. We can't force a difference in others, but we can engage their lives with intention and strategic integrity. This will greatly increase the odds that our action will contribute toward realizing our mission.

Hints for Developing Box E
Action

1. Keep Boxes C and D in view while you design Box E. It might be helpful even to post these two guiding boxes on a wall if a group is working on Box E together to keep the ideas front and center.

2. The first version of Box E can always be upgraded by your Box D. Once you have ideas for a plan, take each plan and try to develop it further by asking how it can better express each notion in your Box D. This process will often increase the effectiveness of your plan and its execution.

3. Develop evaluation tools to assess not only the execution of Box E – *Action*, but also the fidelity of your actions to Boxes A, B, C, and D.

4. Think through who might need a specified articulation of Box E – *Action* to help as a tutor, a mirror, or a cast.

5. Be sure to accompany any behavioral instruction with an explanation of the corresponding ideology that gives the behavior meaning.

PART 3

PRACTICING
AN IDEOLOGY

8. Using the Model—Case study of the RR4CC

I n the Miami-Dade County at the southeast tip of Florida, the county encompassing the expansive and pulsing city of Miami, a group of judges, scholars, attorneys, and community activists gathered together with an idea to improve their community of child welfare professionals. The impulse started with an observation that there was some unevenness in the care that children and families were receiving. Some cases were handled brilliantly, but not all of them. The problem didn't seem to be a lack of effort or good intention; everyone wanted to serve children and families well. Rather, it appeared that for some reason, the findings of research were not being used fully or consistently in welfare practices throughout the region. Case managers, pressed for time and resources, would occasionally make decisions based on instinct and habit, not on what research showed was most effective. They needed a culture change toward evidence-based practice.

Under the illuminative vision and leadership of Judge Cindy Lederman, the group launched an organization called Research and Reform for Children in Court (RR4CC). They agreed to work toward a substantial objective: change the culture of child welfare so thoroughly that every case worker would, by default, turn to research-proven practice regardless of habit, inclination, or ease. But how do you convince the practitioners of multiple agencies throughout a complex professional field and across an expansive and heavily populated county, holding one of the nation's largest and most diverse cities, to change their ways of work? This is a classic challenge of iceberg-moving.

Let's take a look at a few implications of our model to see how it might inform something like the cause of the RR4CC:

1. If we lead below the surface, we exponentially release human potential; if we lead primarily for action or behavior alone, we have little power to move the *status quo*.

Think of the possibilities available to the RR4CC:

··> The board is comprised of some of most esteemed and influential leaders in the child welfare community along with two judges who hold great sway throughout the county. They could try to arm-twist or cajole practitioners into change. Force might work for a while, but it makes durable change tricky. Most likely, new ways would last only as long as the pressure was on. And then, as soon as the board members began to fatigue (as in time they would, for they have their own full lives and professions to lead) old practices would reappear.

··> They could inundate the community with information—studies, case studies, updates via email about recent research findings, stacks of precedents, websites, online libraries and the like. But rarely is anyone's deep practice changed primarily through access to information. We all tend to stay stuck in our ruts and hold onto old habits even when faced with a bounty of reliable information telling us to act differently—just think about how hard it is to eat well, exercise regularly, and get a good night's sleep even though most of us have plenty of access to information about healthy living.

⋯⟩ They could incentivize the process of change by securing grant funds and then doling out money to those agencies that demonstrate an adherence to evidence-based practices. But incentives, when used to get people to do what they do not philosophically embrace, tend to produce a crust of compliance instead of a true and genuine adoption. Practices can be maneuvered to look attractive to funders while surreptitiously masking old habits of thinking. Invariably, the thinking will disempower the practice in the end.

Perhaps some type of pressure, information, and incentive will help advance the cause of the RR4CC. But to establish evidence-based practice, people need to be imbued with evidence-based thinking. They need to value and believe differently (Box B—*Core Convictions*), aim for a different quality of impact (Box C—*Intended Impact*), and become dedicated to the principles behind the practice that make the practices work as they are intended (Box D—*Best Means*). This requires more than merely telling them what to do and getting them to do it.

The benefit of intervening in the ideologies within people is that it also releases a cascade of potential from people. It is the difference between training ("do things this way") and equipping ("here are ways of thinking and tools for creating new and meaningful actions"). This kind of work re-engineers how people engage their profession. For the RR4CC, it is deciding to influence an evidence-based mind-set and not just an evidence-based practice.

What about your case? You have many points of leverage at your fingertips. What tactics might you be tempted to take that would leave you with superficial adjustments instead of genuine transformations? Take a moment and jot down the possibilities available to you, then try to determine which of these engage people above the waterline and which might get down to the values, beliefs, and mind-set below.

2. When we develop ideology within people, we maximize our influence; if we miss developing any part, we risk the chance for change.

Do we *act people into a new way of thinking, or think people into a new way of acting?* Current research suggests that the answer to that question is…yes. To cause change, we have to act our way into new thinking and think our way into new action. The boxes help us bring action and thinking together. This leads us to a key question: Are all of these kinds of ideas important to develop in people, or just some of them? What happens when we overlook one? Let's try it and see.

If we miss **Box C—*Intended Impact,*** we miss the point of the practice. We just do in order to do—to check off our "to do" list, to show our effort, to demonstrate compliance for our board or funders or constituency, or to follow what others have done. But we don't have the intended impact clearly in view. We run hard, but forget what the running is for. We develop what Václav Havel, the former playwright and first post-communist president of the Czech Republic, calls a "cult of action."

In the RR4CC, keeping focused on intended impact keeps everyone from making research or evidence-based practice the end, the main point, the primary achievement. What's the problem with making research the point? Consider this: Research is a means to help children and families thrive. It's a wonderful means, a powerful means, but it is a poor end in itself. If we hold it as an end, we will foment a culture which serves research, instead of a culture using research to improve the welfare of children and families. Many efforts throughout our work—like evaluation, program design, task forces, or even whole departments within our agencies—take on a life of their own and tend to self-perpetuate in service to themselves rather than in service to the impact they were created to make. That's why we need Box C—*Intended Impact.* Box C keeps us thinking about what our actions and strategies are in service to.

If we miss **Box D—*Best Means***, we miss developing the principles behind the practice. We conflate principle with practice and then fail to recognize what makes the practice effective. We get stuck telling people what to do, not why *this kind* of doing is more effective than other kinds. When we can identify the principles behind the practice, however, our practice becomes properly animated. Without it, the execution of a practice, even a best practice, is often empty of effect. Or, we lock onto a particular practice and refuse, over time, to adjust it or let it go.

For the RR4CC, the ideas in this box are about how a professional community best changes its ways. When the board of the RR4CC considers possible strategies, they will have them vetted by the principles of this theory of change. They will resist the temptation simply to brainstorm and throw programs at the county's welfare community in hope that something will stick. They will even resist the temptation simply to copy the practices of organizations with a similar mission. Instead, they will learn and model from other organizations' successes instead of mimic. And the development of their tactics will be guided by an underlying theory of community change, a good Box D—*Best Means*.

If we miss **Box B—*Premises*** (*Context and Core Convictions*), we fail to understand readiness for change, the influence of the environment, and the rival priorities of others that are pulling in opposing directions. If we misdiagnose premises of beliefs, we may flail against unseen sources of intractability. And if we miss renovating, or at least influencing, the core convictions within people, we may activate an immunity response from within their existing ideology that will render our efforts futile.

The RR4CC will need to determine what currents are pulling on the deeper parts of their profession's iceberg. If, as Ron Heifetz and Marty Linsky of Harvard's Kennedy School of Government explain, "every system is perfectly designed to achieve the results it is getting," they will need to ascertain how the environment is supporting the behavior they seek to change. They will also need to discern what notions people currently believe and what *cherished theories* they hold and assume to be true. If they can see into Box B—*Premises*, they will know where and how best to intervene.

If we miss **Box A—*Ultimate Aims***, we may fail to practice what we preach. For the RR4CC, it means that they will be evidence-based in their own approach to change. This requires a certain commitment to self-reflection, openness to scrutiny, transparency in process and agenda, and respectful curiosity regarding all points of data. These are the values of research. And these will need to be modeled by the RR4CC to secure them in others and not just promulgate them to others.

What about your case? Take a moment and think about what ideas might belong in each of your Boxes, and what might belong in the Boxes of those you work with? How might you discern the ideologies of those you are seeking to serve?

3. If we help people hold ideas rightly, we increase the power of the ideas; if we misplace ideas, even good ones, we stand in our own way and inhibit the development of others.

How we hold ideas, not just what ideas we hold, matters. We can imagine that it's enough to have good ideas, that it doesn't matter how we hold them, or where they sit in our ideological frame, as long as the ideas we have are good ideas. Our model helps us see, however, that we must hold our good ideas rightly, not simply hold them. This means that where we place the idea—in which box we position it—has consequences. A good idea, held wrongly, has a surprisingly corrosive tendency. Before we turn to the case of the RR4CC, let's take a look at a couple of illustrations and see if we can spot the possible consequences of a good, but misplaced idea:

The Community-School Partnership (C-SP) in Surrey, a sprawling suburb just southeast and across a rip of water from Vancouver, British Columbia, exists to improve the achievement of children within the Surrey community. Surrey is about as complex as communities get. In recent years it's grown quickly—partially because of an influx of immigrants and refugees—and has become more populated than any other suburb, rivaling even Vancouver in size. The staff members of the C-SP believe in the powerful idea of building a web of partnerships between the school and other local resources—families, agencies, and civic programs—in service to the achievement of children.

The idea of partnering is fundamental to the Community-School Partnership—hence the name, Community-School *Partnership.* Partnering is a very good idea. But what would happen if we held it in a Box C—*Intended Impact,* as if partnering were the end, not the means? We would then tend to build partnerships at any cost and sometimes even at the expense of impacting the lives of children. We may become so intent on forging alliances and starting joint ventures and signing new partners that we forget what it is all in service to. The aim is not to have a partnership, but to impact children. A partnership is helpful only insofar as it accomplishes that end. Some partnerships might even inhibit progress toward that end. The idea can't be held healthily in Box C.

Or, what would happen if the idea of partnerships were held as a Box A—*Ultimate Aims*? In all things, then, we would seek to partner, regardless of quality, common vision, congruent strategies, or any other philosophical consideration. It would matter less how we carried ourselves as a partner, or what power we were exploiting in the partnership, or who we chose to let in the partnership (except that none should be left out!), only that at the end of the day we had many partners. This could prove disastrous for the mission. Collaboration is a great idea. But if it is held wrongly, it is damaging. The idea of partnering makes a wonderful and powerful Box D—*Best Means,* but should not be held as Box C—*Intended Impact* or Box A—*Ultimate Aims*.

Consider another example in a much larger and complex human system—a nation. How does a society hold its good ideas? Just for illustration, let's take the idea of an election, a cherished idea of Western civilization. Democratic societies believe in elections because elections secure a representative form of governance for a citizenry. But where should we hold the very good idea of an election? And does it matter?

Where would you place an idea like *election* within the ideological iceberg? Is it a Box A, where we say, "In all things we will have elections"? This could get us into trouble, promoting elections in regions of the world where this particular expression of self-determination is not yet possible for a variety of cultural or societal reasons. Is it a Box C—*Intended Impact*? In that case, our mission would be to promote elections, and as long as we hold an election we attained our mission. That's it. Is it our Box D—*Best Means*? If so, then we have no other way of advocating for representation or self-determination or participation or self-governance other than holding an election.

Perhaps *election* is one good Box E—*Action*, one way in which we can express our Box D—*Best Means* notion of democracy and the democratic processes of public responsibility, representation, and self-governance? And can we hold onto the idea of elections as one Box E—*Action* among many ideas designed to promote a Box C—*Intended Impact* of liberty, agency, self-determination, and citizenry? And can it be one expression of our Box B—*Core Convictions* about the inalienable rights of every human being in a society? And can we "show up" embodying the Box A—*Ultimate Aims* to respect the dignity of humankind in all things and at all times while promoting elections. How we hold ideas matters.

For the RR4CC, the great idea of "evidence-based practice" is placed in Box E—*Action*, motivated by the values of research and disciplined reflection in Box D—*Best Means* and in service to a particular kind of Box C—*Intended Impact* within the community. Pursuing a practice, no matter how wonderful, should not become the Box A—*Ultimate Aims* at the expense of the modeling and authentic essence of those leading the charge.

What about your case? Take a moment to consider if there are good ideas that might be held poorly by you or others. For this exercise, try to avoid binary, good idea/bad idea thinking. Rather, see if some good ideas are being held poorly and try to anticipate how misplacing a good idea might inadvertently compromise your iceberg-moving impact.

4. If we can intervene in the deeper parts of people, we have a chance of promoting true change; if we simply tinker with the behavior, we might end up causing more resistance.

As you might imagine, many of us feel a strong impulse to pay attention solely to the surface of our effort. At times, the urge is irresistible, and understandably so. We want to touch what we work with. We want to see tangible and measurable effects. We want something concrete to hold and something solid to give others. We feel responsible to demonstrate hard evidence to our board, our staff, our clients and constituency. But a belief is hard to touch. A way of thinking is difficult to count. Ideas like "meaning" and "culture" are tricky to measure. The "sense around here" is tough to discern or defend in concrete, unambiguous terms. Hence, we tend to fixate on Box E—*Action*.

However, any effort to cause change merely by manipulating surface elements may make the current situation even more stubborn and resistant, an ironic twist in the pursuit of difference-making. This is because human systems are sensitive and dynamically balanced to sustain a stasis of equilibrium. They are designed to recover from anything that threatens to cause imbalance or disequilibration. A human system, in other words, though remarkably adaptable on the surface, doesn't like to be disturbed in its essence. Our tinkering with the surface sometimes makes the problem worse.

Robert Kegan, a quick-witted and affable psychologist and educator from Harvard University, has spent a career studying the ways human beings develop. He uses the parlance of *immunity to change* as a way to describe the resistance people and groups of people exhibit when pushed to develop. The metaphor is an intriguing one.

Think about the physiology of an individual, a human system of one. How does a body keep itself from disease? When working properly, a force of physiological equilibrium is extraordinarily effective in saving us from dangerous bacteria, viruses, and toxins. As soon as it detects some threat, an immune system launches an all-out defense. It identifies, attacks, and neutralizes the offending antigens. Most of the time, thankfully, infection is thwarted and the threat of disease is extinguished quickly and efficiently. Then, our systems can return to their normal, healthy selves and we can go on with our normal, healthy lives. The immunity response is a startling, effective way to retain and protect equilibrium throughout the human body.

What about a non-biological human system that needs to be changed—say a branch office, a call center, the faculty of a college, a family, or even a community? What if one of those human systems has settled into an unhealthy equilibrium that we actually *want* to infect and disequilibrate for the good? What if we intentionally want to disrupt the stasis of a human system? An immunity response, similar to the one keeping us physically healthy, is at work. Just as with our biology, any effort to transform a human system will activate a virulent immunity response from the system, a response bent on neutralizing our efforts and wiping out our influence.

Systems of human equilibrium are sensitive and remarkably adept at self-balancing, even if they are stuck in a malformed state. To explain this in terms of our Boxes and iceberg, tinkering with Box E usually initiates a powerful immunity response from Boxes A, B, C, and D, and nothing much, in the end, is moved. In a human body, the only way to alter the equilibrium is either to overwhelm or disarm the immune system. The same holds true for the people and organizations we want to turn around. It explains how true difference-making by trying to change the action alone is so elusive.

The metaphor of immunity also suggests, even more curiously, that people can be inoculated against change, and that a human organization can be complicit in establishing and maintaining the system holding people to an unhealthy status quo. In other words, there are reasons things are as they are. Some reasons are the result of our superficial efforts to change without engaging the deeper parts of people. The situation is stuck even with clear opportunity and instruction to move forward. Without under-the-surface intervention, the ideology of the status quo will overpower and outmaneuver any attempt to move a part of a person, department, organization, or community. Since every organization is a human system at its core, a biological notion like immunity is a powerfully heuristic way to think about what we are up against. The key, then, will be to find a way to intervene in the underlying parts of the system—those positions of value, fear, assumption, and belief.

In light of the challenge facing the RR4CC, this point about immunity is critical. It highlights the importance of anticipating immunity responses that will be roused by interventions. RR4CC won't be able to just provide a convincing alternative and expect that people will adopt it. The immunity response will be too powerful.

Growth and develoment, then, will require some loss, some "giving up" of what the constituents have been gaining from the old system—a dearly held belief, a kind of comfort in the stasis, a certain feeling of expertise, a cherished sense of personal identity that "since I've been doing this for a long time I know what I'm doing," and the like. Getting people to identify their anticipated loss, helping them unpack the core beliefs attached to that loss, and then recasting the vision of what might be gained by letting go will help illuminate how the force of immunity might be neutralized.

What about your case? Where are there points of resistance? What kinds of assumptions, beliefs, and conclusions might be giving rise to the immunity responses you sense in others? For a moment, try to identify what you anticipate is holding people from growing and developing.

Judge Lederman and the directors of the Research and Reform for Children in Court recognize that to change the behavior of welfare practitioners, they must also concurrently change the mind-set of welfare practitioners. One expression of their Box E—*Action* is to gather critical community leaders and executive directors of key agencies and talk about the ideas of Boxes A, B, C, and D and together develop strategies to embed the ideas within their region's practitioners to provoke changes in the culture of the child welfare system. The directors of RR4CC have resisted the impulse simply to provide best practices, train new techniques, incentivize performance, or make a public call for compliance. These fine strategies might be adopted as supporting measures in time, but at this point, since they want to provoke both transformational and durable change, they are deliberately diving into the current and needed ideologies ingrained in the welfare community and renovating the approaches of their constituencies. They are designing interventions that are both practical and ideological. They are working to *act people into thinking differently* and *to think people into acting differently*. It is change in both action and thinking—both sides of the waterline for their iceberg—and holds promise for the future of child welfare in Miami-Dade County.

9. Using the Model—Examples in Practice

We have been on a journey together through these pages, thinking about how to leverage ideas in service to the growth and development of people and the human systems that hold them. I realize that the nature of this work requires a commitment over time for each of us to gain the skills needed to intervene with people below the waterline of their thinking. Very few of us pick it up quickly. But to see progress in one's ability to see and engage the whole of human systems is thrilling. This is meaningful work.

Sometimes, it takes seeing an example of another who is along in this journey to be encouraged and inspired. A growing group of people are applying these ideas to the human icebergs in their professions and lives, and some of their stories are fascinating. Lara used the model to help her mother navigate a professional transition and gain a strategy for her future role and place of contribution. Josh has applied it both professionally in his role as nonprofit executive director and personally in his role as husband. Kate has utilized the model to coach colleagues and those she supervises in her organization as well as to help a local public school administration develop strategy for closing the achievement gap in their region.

There are other fascinating and inspiring accounts. This approach is being used in personal and professional roles, in domestic and international initiatives, in nonprofit and corporate ventures, in endeavors large and small.

Log on to www.dialogueboxes.com to read vignettes written by those who are on the front lines, applying the model to their lives and work. You will see how the model works from their points of view and in their context. If you find your own application, you are invited to add your story.

Bibliography

Introduction

Rucker, Philip. 2008. "United Way to Target Health, Education and Income." *Washington Post,* May 15.

Chapter 2

Eisner, Elliot. 1979. *The Educational Imagination.* New York: Macmillan.

Frankena, William. 1965. *Philosophy of Education.* New York: MacMillan.

Chapter 3

Frankl, Victor. 1997. *Man's Search for Meaning.* New York: Pocket Books.

Havel, Václav. 1992. *Open Letters: Selected Writings, 1965-1990,* p. 231. New York: Vintage Press.

Chapter 4

Cooperrider, David. 2005. *Appreciative Inquiry: A Positive Revolution in Change.* San Francisco, CA: Berrett-Koehler Publishers.

Kegan, Robert. 1982. *The Evolving Self: Problem and Process in Human Development.* Cambridge, MA: Harvard University Press.

Whitehead, Alfred North. 1967. *The Aims of Education and Other Essays.* New York: Free Press.

Chapter 5

Albany Nonviolent Movement. "Handbill," 1998. In *Debating the Civil Rights Movement, 1945-1968,* edited by **Steven F. Lawson** and **Charles Payne**, p. 141. Lanham, Maryland: Rowman & Littlefield.

Chapter 5 *(continued)*

The Student Nonviolent Coordinating Committee (as revised in conference, April 29, 1962). *The Charles Sherrod Papers, file 24,* State Historical Society of Wisconsin.

Holland, Kelley. 2007. *"The Workplace: Revising the Strategy of Mission Statements." Illustrations of Microsoft, American Standard, and Estee Lauder.* International Herald Tribune, Sept 24. Chapter 7

Senge, Peter. 2006. *The Fifth Disicpline: The Art and Practice of the Learning Organization.* New York, NY: Crown Business Business.

Cooperrider, David. 2005. *Appreciative Inquiry: A Positive Revolution in Change.* San Francisco, CA: Berrett-Koehler Publishers.

Chapter 8

Heifetz, Ronald, and **Martin Linsky.** 2002. *Leadership on the Line: Staying Alive through the Dangers of Leadership.* Cambridge, MA: Harvard Business School Press.

Kegan, Robert, and **Lisa Lahey.** 2009. *Immunity to Change: How to Overcome It and Unlock the Potential in Yourself and Your Organization.* Cambridge, MA: Harvard Business School Press.

Havel, Václav. 1992. *Open Letters: Selected Writings, 1965-1990.* New York: Vintage Press.